HEROES
OF THE FAITH

ADVICE FROM GOD'S ATHLETES

ELLIOT JOHNSON

CROSS TRAINING
PUBLISHING

HEROES OF THE FAITH

Copyright © 1999 by Cross Training Publishing

Library of Congress Cataloging-in-Publication Data

ISBN 1-887002-26-X
Johnson, Elliot
Elliot Johnson

HEROES OF THE FAITH / Elliot Johnson
Published by Cross Training Publishing, Grand Island, Nebraska
68803

Distributed in the United States and Canada by Cross Training
Publishing

Unless otherwise indicated, all Scripture quotations are from the *Holy Bible, New International Version,* © 1973, 1978, 1984, International Bible Society. Used by permission of Zondervan Bible Publishers. Other quotations are taken from *New American Standard Bible,* (NASB) © The Lockman Foundation 1960, 1962, 1963,1968, 1971,1972, 1973, 1975, 1977, the *Revised Standard Version of the Bible* (RSV) © 1946, 1952, 1971,1973, the *Authorized/King James Version* (KJV).

Cover illustrator: Jeff Sharpton
Printed in the United States of America

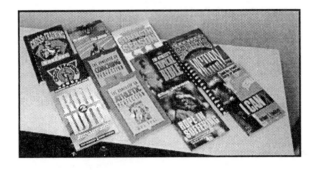

For additional books and resources
available through Cross Training
Publishing contact us at:
Cross Training Publishing
P.O. Box 1541
Grand Island, NE 68802
(308) 384-5762

CONTENTS

PREFACE

First Corinthians 10:1–13 tells us that what occurred in the lives of the Old Testament saints happened as examples for us. In the New Testament, we see men and women facing essentially the same struggles that we face in the twentieth century. Although they were not confronted with athletic eligibility conflicts, traffic jams, or problems with the microwave, they did struggle with ostracism because of their commitment to Christ, problems of big government in the Roman Empire, and living morally in an immoral world. The principles are the same now as then, and I have learned much about God's dealing with people in studying the lives of these *Heroes of Faith*. May you and I become more successful in the game of life as we become more conformed each day to the image of Jesus Christ.

Elliot Johnson

ACKNOWLEDGMENTS

With sincere appreciation to:

Our Lord and Savior, Jesus Christ
Judy, a loving wife
Esther, a prayerful mother
Sam Sample, Buddy Martin, Steve Robinson, Doug Henry

. . . and all others who care enough to pray for the athletes and coaches who use sports as a vehicle to share the Good News of Jesus Christ.

INTRODUCTION

In athletic competition, some plays must be initiated that are not based on what appears, but based on the assurance of the desired result. For example, a quarterback often releases the football before the receiver breaks in the direction of the throw. Or, a catcher throws directly to second base on a steal attempt, trusting the infielder to be at the bag when the throw arrives. A fast-break pass in basketball is often based on a sense of where a teammate will be at a certain time. Each of these plays requires faith, as well as skill.

God's Word defines faith as our "being sure of what we hope for and certain of what we do not see" (Heb. 11:1). It is God's plan that we live by faith, believing that God exists and that He rewards us when we seek Him (Heb. 11:6). In the Old Testament, God asked men to live by faith and then He commended them in the New Testament (Heb. 11:2). In fact, the eleventh chapter of Hebrews is God's Hall of Fame, recounting great exploits and victories for God by men of faith.

Interestingly, the more we examine the lives of these heroes, the less we venerate them. But in spite of their character flaws, a sovereign, omnipotent God was able to use them to accomplish His will in their time. What a hope for us in days of uncertainty and unrest! As we study these heroes, who experienced not only great successes but also great failures, we will learn to appreciate their lives and God's role in making heroes from ordinary men and women of faith.

Despite the extraordinary exploits of God's heroes over thousands of years, the Old Testament closes without the revelation of the greatest hero of all, the promised Messiah. The last book ends with a curse: Israel is under a law they cannot keep, and the heavens are silent as God goes off the air for four hundred years.

Then suddenly, dramatically, and perfectly timed, the Father split the atmosphere with the joyful news that His Son had become human—a baby born to a virgin teenager named Mary. God's greatest hero lay in a Bethlehem stable; His arrival celebrated by myriads of angels but by relatively few perceptive men. His was a normal childhood in Nazareth—being reared in a poor carpenter's home amid at least four brothers and two sisters, learning to speak and read fluently, observing the creation He Himself had made, working, studying, and praying. No more is known of His early years. But the stage was being set. The Romans ruled the world, providing a measure of peace for the Prince of Peace to do His work. The exacting Greek language remained nearly universal and proved ideal to record His teachings. The religious emptiness and futility of the Jewish laws left men with a hunger to know the living God who would change the calendars of the world. God had scheduled His arrival, and Jesus Christ kept His date with destiny.

More volumes have been written about Jesus than any other man. More lives have been touched for the better because of His birth, life, death, and resurrection than could possibly be counted. Because of the Son of God, the entire history of the world has been altered. None of the lives of God's other heroes compare remotely with the perfection of the Lord Jesus. He stands alone, above and beyond the lives of man's greatest politicians, military leaders, and religious heroes. Jesus Christ not only sits at the right hand of almighty God, but He lives in the hearts of all who will have Him as personal Lord and Savior. In the New Testament, we see Him performing even greater works (John 14:12) through the lives of those who live after Calvary—more ordinary men and women whose lives were changed because of His life. May your life be similarly touched as you study God's newborn heroes.

Playing by the Rules

The Lord looked with favor on Abel and his offering.   Gen. 4:4

Yankee batting instructor Dick Sisler has gained respect as one of the most knowledgeable hitting coaches in baseball. He has saved many careers and helped players go on to play baseball at higher levels. One young man, however, came to Dick after his release from pro-ball and lamented, "If only I had listened to you and done things your way, my career might have been saved. I should have done what you said." Doubtless, others have learned this same hard lesson: Human nature is insistent on *its own way.*

Cain was one of those people who should have done things God's way. While Abel came to the Lord with a blood sacrifice to symbolize the atonement of a coming Savior for his sins, Cain brought the fruit of his own efforts to pacify God. He was like so many people who come with good works, baptism, reformed ways and say to God, "You can accept me now because the good I'm doing is balancing out my sins." But no one is saved unless he comes to God on His terms—a broken spirit with confession of sin and faith in Jesus Christ as God's perfect sacrifice. There is no other way (John 14:6). Abel came trusting God and found forgiveness. Hebrews 11:4 tells us that by faith Abel offered the better sacrifice and was commended as righteous. He became a hero of faith based on his trust in God. Cain came trusting his own efforts and found judgment; then he became jealous and murdered his brother.

Rather than come to God on your own merit, you must realize that He has designed a plan for you to reach heaven by confessing your sin and believing on the Lord Jesus Christ as your atoning sacrifice. Listen and heed His call now.

Consider: *Why is there only one way to be saved?*

A Record of Consistency

Enoch walked with God; then he was no more, because God took him away.   Gen. 5:24

For his consistency in hitting, Joe DiMaggio was outstanding. The Yankee Clipper is probably best remembered for hitting in fifty-six consecutive games in 1941. He also had the second longest minor-league streak, once hitting in sixty-one straight games for the San Francisco Seals. These records for performance will be difficult to eclipse.

For his consistency in walking with God, Enoch was outstanding. Though not much is recorded about the life of this hero of faith, he is remembered as one who pleased God with such consistency that God took him directly to heaven without dying. That record will also be difficult to beat!

Notice what is recorded about Enoch. In Genesis 5, where the life spans of the ancients are given (men lived longer before the worldwide flood drastically changed the earth's surface and atmospheric conditions), Enoch is commended for "walking with God" (vv. 22, 24). Hebrews 11:5 records that he "pleased God" and that "by faith" he left this life. Jude 14 tells us he prophesied, and Luke 3: 37 records that Enoch was a direct ancestor of Joseph, who watched over the Lord Jesus as He grew up.

What does it mean to *walk with God?* First, it means being redeemed from the curse of sin by faith in Jesus Christ; then being constantly aware of His presence and living as if He is watching; finally talking to God, listening to Him, obeying His Word, and making His priorities your priorities, so your life brings glory to Him. How's your walk today?

Consider: *Does how you live influence how you die?*

An Unusual Way to Win

Noah found favor (grace) in the eyes of the Lord.   Gen. 6:8

Austrian skier Toni Sailer had his preparations for the 1956 Olympic Downhill Alpine Ski Race interrupted just before the race. As he tightened the straps of his skis, one strap broke. He couldn't find a spare strap until Hansl Senger, trainer of the Italian team, noticed the panic in the Austrian team. Senger graciously took the straps from his own ski bindings and gave them to Sailer, who won the race.

Many years ago, God interrupted the violence and corruption of mankind with judgment on the entire earth. All mankind was doomed, separated from God by sin and rebellion. So, a holy God justly declared the first rainout, since Genesis tells us that previously the earth had been watered only by surface water. At that time, only one man walked with God—Noah (v. 9). God gave Noah specific directions for an ark of safety and as he preached for 120 years warning men of judgment, he worked on the gigantic vessel. Though others ignored his message until the very day he entered the ark (Luke 17:27), Noah did all God told him to do by faith, which still speaks to us today (Heb. 11:7).

Our God was even more gracious than Hansl Senger, because He provided an ark of safety for all who would enter. The ark represents the Lord Jesus Christ—our ark of safety from the penalty of sin. As Noah found favor by believing God, we, too, can trust Christ and ignore the scoffing of nonbelievers and be delivered from eternal punishment in hell. God has always made a way for those who trust Him by faith (2 Peter 2:4–9)—the Lord Jesus Christ.

Consider: *How important is a right relationship with God?*

A Multiyear Contract

On that day the Lord made a covenant with Abram. . . .   Gen 15:18

Four-time Cy Young Award winner Steve Carlton was known as baseball's most effective pitcher and highest paid pitcher at over one million dollars per year. Steve and the Philadelphia Phillies had a legally binding agreement concerning his services and his remuneration that could not be changed except by mutual consent of both parties. In today's era of broken contracts, free agents, and inflated salaries, it is not widely known that in 1973, after a 13–20 season, he asked the Phils to *reduce* his salary. Not many of today's athletes would ask to renegotiate that way; none are legally required to.

God's relationship to man is also based on a covenant—a binding agreement. In Genesis 15, God made a covenant with Abram and promised to give him land and a son to inherit all that he possessed. Then, He foretold some astonishing future events in the lives of His people Israel. Finally, He sealed the promise in the customary manner of the times. Dead animals were split in half, and the covenant partners passed between the halves, which meant "may the Lord do to me as these animals if I violate this agreement." God caused a smoking fire pot (symbolizing Israel's Egyptian bondage) and a blazing torch (symbolizing His light of comfort) to pass between the pieces.

As God gave Abram a righteous standing with Himself, He established an equally inviolate contract with believers today. The guarantee of our salvation is signed, sealed, and delivered by none other than the Lord Jesus Christ. His split body on Calvary insured salvation for all believers, which was the significance of "It is finished" when He died. No true believer would ever want to renegotiate this multiyear contract (eternity), which can't really be renegotiated and pays only the highest benefits.

Consider: *If God saves you, who keeps you saved?*

Inconsistent Hero

. . . and there Abraham said of his wife Sarah, "She is my sister." Gen. 20:2

Like many longtime ball hitters, Reggie Jackson has one glaring weakness—he strikes out often. Though ranking as one of the greatest sluggers in baseball history, Reggie has been inconsistent in making contact with the ball. In 1983, he became the first major leaguer to fan two thousand times in his career. His greatness is tempered by his inconsistency.

Abraham lived like Reggie Jackson hits: He was inconsistent. Though more lines are written about Abraham, the "father of faith," than any other hero of faith in Hebrews 11, there were times when he did not trust God. By faith Abraham left his home in Ur, but in unbelief he went down to Egypt (Gen. 12). By faith he rescued Lot (Gen. 14), but in unbelief he lied about Sarah (Gen. 12). By faith he believed God's promise of an heir (Gen. 15), but in unbelief he tried to do things his own way through Hagar (Gen. 16). By faith he offered Isaac to God (Gen. 22), but in unbelief he lied to Abimelech (Gen. 20). In this last story, we see that Abraham purposed in his heart from the very time he left Ur to tell a half-truth (a lie) about his wife (Sarah was his half-sister) because he feared for his life (vv. 11–13).

Notice how God in His sovereign plan protected Abraham and returned Sarah to him. There was really no reason for Abraham to lie when the Lord had everything under control. Abraham could have saved himself much grief by trusting the Lord in every situation because God had it all worked out. Nevertheless, the Word of God is honest about its heroes, so in studying their shortcomings we see our own.

How much does your walk of faith resemble Abraham's? God holds the lives of believers in the palm of His hand, so we need not worry or take matters into our own hands.

Consider: *What does God's sovereignty mean to you?*

How to Avoid Burnout

Abraham   Read Genesis 22

"Now I know that you fear God, because you have not withheld from me your son, your only son."   Gen. 22:12

The coaching profession has coined a new term to explain the recent early retirement of so many great coaches. It's called "coaching burnout" and results from endless hours of planning, preparation, and competition. Though describing the coaching profession as "harder now than it used to be," Coach Tom Landry exhibits no signs of coaching burnout.

"If football was the number one thing in your life, and if you lived with that pressure all the time, I could understand burnout," said Landry. "Football is not the number one thing with me. My priorities are different from others—not that I don't work as hard as any other coach—but a Christian life is the most important thing to me."

Abraham must have had similar priorities in his life. Scripture tells the story of how God tested him to see just what was more important—obeying God or the physical life of his own son, the heir of all he possessed and the hope of future generations. Abraham didn't understand, but he obeyed, proving that no person or possession would stand between him and his God. In passing this test, Abraham experienced the feelings of God Himself, who sent His only Son, Jesus Christ, to die for us. As God provided the lamb for Abraham to substitute for the life of Isaac, so Christ was the sacrificial Lamb in our place. The obedience of Isaac is a picture of the perfect obedience of the Lord Jesus to His Father's will.

Hebrews 11:17–19 tells us that Abraham offered his son by faith, knowing that God was able to raise him up if He desired. He became a hero of faith by trusting God. Could you pass such a test? Do you trust God enough to give Him the best of all you have?

Consider: *If God doesn't have your best, who does?*

Persistence Pays Off

Jacob   Read Genesis 32:22–31

"... you have struggled with God and with men and have overcome."
Gen. 32:28

In 1982, an East Carolina linebacker named Gerry Rogers finally played in a game for the first time since 1978. His is a remarkable record of persistence. The Pennsylvania All-Star went to Maryland but did not play and transferred to Villanova. Once there he had to sit out a year because of the transfer. Villanova then dropped football the following year. Gerry went to East Carolina and contracted mononucleosis, causing him to sit out another year. In early 1982, after working his way to the top of the depth chart, he broke his hand and missed the first half of the season. His endurance was finally rewarded late in 1982. Not many players would have persisted under such adversity.

The man Jacob ("schemer") had many character flaws. But one of the positive aspects of his life was the persistence he showed during an unbelievable all-night struggle to gain God's blessing. During the incredible struggle, Jacob wept and pleaded with God (Hos. 12:4) as he aggressively sought the Lord's blessing on his life. After this severe struggle, Jacob received a new name— Israel—and a different character. Physically, Jacob won the match, but his hip was supernaturally dislocated, causing Jacob to remember that he was to be dependent on God. He was never the same again. Now having found power with the Lord in prayer, he became powerful among men. His persistence with God was rewarded.

You'll never be something for God in public until you get right with God in private. It takes time alone with God to listen for His voice, to receive instruction from the Master, to gain a renewed mind for the day.

Consider: *How do you know when you have contacted God?*

Knowing When to Say No!

Joseph   Read Genesis 39

But he left his cloak in her hand and ran out of the house.   Gen. 39:12

Texas Christian University's head football coach Jim Wacker could have easily swept a problem under the rug during the 1985 season when he discovered that several star players had received money illegally from boosters of the TCU program. But instead of yielding to the temptation to enjoy a big season and a bowl appearance dishonestly, Wacker took a stand with a resounding No! He dismissed several key athletes and turned over information about the payoffs to the NCAA. Though his win-loss record suffered, he was a big winner in God's eyes.

It is always better to be honest and suffer than to continue for the sake of "saving face." Joseph was another man in such a predicament. Though he had earned trust as a servant of high moral character, Joseph was incessantly bombarded with temptation to sin sexually. Day after day (v. 10) his master's alluring wife propositioned him. But wise Joseph knew sin when he smelled it and knew of its terrible consequences. He may have realized that those involved in adultery ofen end up hating both themselves and their partner. As much as possible, he refused to go near the woman. Finally, she grabbed him to pull him to bed. Rather than stick around and increase the temptation, Joseph ran. Though he later suffered for doing right, God was with him. Through wisdom that included moral purity, Joseph later became prime minister of the entire Egyptian nation.

What about your moral character? Do you have the resolve of a Jim Wacker or a Joseph? Before temptation ever comes, determine to maintain moral integrity. When it does come, don't let pride keep you from escaping a situation that can only hurt all involved. Though we need not fear problems, we must flee from temptation.

Consider: *How often do you flee temptation?*

Why Can't Life Be Fair?

Joseph   Read Genesis 45

"So then, it was not you who sent me here, but God."   Gen. 45:8

Andy McGaffigan of the Montreal Expos was a rising star in the Yankees' organization before being traded. At the time of the trade, he said: "I've been in the game long enough to know this happens, but when it happened to me, all of a sudden I was anxious. There were a lot of questions in my mind and I didn't know the answers. One day I was the big prospect; the next day I was gone. If I had not known the Lord at that time, they would have had to lock me up. The night of the trade I . . . read Romans 8:28, and all of my questions were answered. Confidence began to flow back into my soul. It was God's Holy Spirit pouring through me, making me ready for whatever was to come. Praise the Lord." God meant everything for good in Andy's life, and now he has stuck with Montreal.

The life of Joseph could be summed up in these same words, "God meant it for good." Joseph had been betrayed by his jealous brothers and sold into slavery in Egypt (Gen. 37), had been trained by God through the adversity of undeserved punishment in prison (Gen. 39), and finally had been elevated to prime minister of all Egypt (Gen. 41). When his brothers came seeking food, they didn't realize they were bowing down to Joseph to fulfill an old dream (Gen. 42). When Joseph finally revealed himself to them (Gen. 45), he wasn't bitter and didn't seek the revenge he so easily could have taken; rather, he saw things from God's perspective. He said, "It was not you who sent me here, but God." Later, he repeated God's perspective. "You intended to harm me, but God intended it for good to accomplish what is now being done, the saving of many lives" (Gen. 50:20).

Are you going through a struggle you do not understand? Remember Joseph. None of God's other heroes suffered so unfairly. But God used it all to bring good in the end.

Consider: *How can you apply Romans 8:28 to your life?*

What's That in Your Hand?

Moses   Read Exodus 3:1—4:5

"But take this staff in your hand so you can perform miraculous signs with it."
Exod. 4:17

It is amazing that God uses perishable objects to bring honor and glory to Himself. The glove, bat, helmet, or racket of a Christian athlete can be used for the glory of God and the good of others as he or she presents it to the Father. Managers or coaches can trust God to use their position of influence to bring others to Christ. What a privilege for the believer to be used by the Lord!

Moses was wandering on the backside of a desert when God got his attention by appearing in a burning bush. The Lord said, "I have seen . . . I have heard . . . I am concerned . . . so I have come . . . to rescue my people from Egyptian bondage." God had chosen Moses to deliver His people. When Moses balked, God asked for the common shepherd's staff he carried, the symbol of his care and protection of his sheep as well as a support for walking. All God asked of Moses was to "throw it down" (4:3). Once Moses did, it was never the same old staff again. First, it became a snake, a sign to Moses and later to the entire Egyptian nation of God's call to Moses. When he stretched it across the Red Sea, the waters parted. When he struck a rock in the desert, water flowed from it. Although not magical or powerful in itself, Moses' staff was used by God to accomplish His purpose in the lives of millions of people.

What is in your hand? A baseball bat? A tennis racket? A football helmet? A golf club? If you'll give it to God, subordinate your desires and priorities to the one goal of pleasing God, He will take that tool and use it. It will never be just the same old piece of sports equipment again. As you trust Christ, it will be a vehicle through which you can communicate God's love to others. When committed to the Lord, your God-given hobby or profession can bring much glory to God and good to others.

Consider: *What can you give to God?*

Composure Under Pressure

Moses   Read Exodus 14

"Do not be afraid. Stand firm and you will see the deliverance the Lord will bring you today."   Exod. 14:13

Allie Reynolds was one of the few pitchers to hurl two no-hitters in the same season (1951). The second one he threw is remarkable because in the bottom of the ninth inning, catcher Yogi Berra dropped Ted Williams's foul pop-up to give new life to the Red Sox slugger. Undaunted, Reynolds then induced Williams to hit another pop-up that Berra caught. Reynolds's composure under pressure helped him complete the game, where another pitcher might have become frustrated and lost his poise.

Moses also demonstrated composure under pressure when he led Israel out of Egyptian bondage. Hundreds of thousands of Jews had just seen God's wrath on their enemies (ten plagues on Egypt). With the Egyptian army in hot pursuit and the sea blocking their escape, they became fearful and complaining (vv. 10–12). In the crisis, Moses obeyed God and stretched out his rod to part the sea. Hebrews 11:29 tells us that by faith the people stepped onto the dry sea floor, passed through, and then saw the entire army of Egypt drowned in the collapsing waters. The crossing of the Red Sea became one of the most dramatic, far-reaching manifestations of God's power in the Old Testament and provides us with a picture of our salvation by God's grace through faith.

Do you realize that a crisis is necessary to apply faith? If everything were going smoothly in our lives, we'd have no opportunity to demonstrate faith. When faced with uncertainty, we have the chance to trust God, and He is glorified through our trust and His deliverance of us. He is trustworthy in every trial we face.

Consider: *What crisis has God allowed to prove your faith?*

Visions of Greatness

Moses   Read Exodus 33:18–23

". . . I will cause all my goodness to pass in front of you. . . ."   Exod. 33:19

In the 1968 Olympic Games in Mexico City, as *Reader's Digest* reports, Bob Beamon made a lasting impression of excellence with one incredible long jump. The world long-jump record had stood at 27'4 3/4". The high-flying Beamon sailed an unbelievable 29'2 1/2"—almost two *feet* beyond the record. When his distance was announced, Beamon fell to his knees with his hands over his face. Russian long-jumper Igor Ter-Ovanesyan commented to American Ralph Boston, "Compared to that, the rest of us are children."

Spiritually, all of us need a fresh vision of God's power in our lives. Seeing His greatness makes our problems seem small and keeps us from getting discouraged by this depressing world.

Moses, a great hero of faith, prayed on behalf of God's people (Exod. 33). He asked that God Himself go with the people into the Promised Land. Still, Moses needed to be reminded of God's greatness and power, so he asked to see His glory. He needed a fresh vision of God to encourage and strengthen his faith.

Notice how God responds: "You cannot see my face, for no man can see me and live" (v. 20). Although he could not see the *essence* of God, since God is so holy that Moses couldn't stand it, God did allow Moses to see a *manifestation* of His glory by looking after God had passed by him. Possibly it was like the visual impression that is left on the brain after seeing a flash of lightning: Your mind's eye still sees the flash after you close your eyes. Regardless, Moses' faith was strengthened.

Do you need a fresh vision of God's power and greatness? Jesus Christ is the manifestation of God. His exalted position reminds us of the authority of God over all evil. One look at Him will put all problems in proper perspective.

Consider: *How can you see God manifested today?*

24

Putting Aside Personal Advancement

Moses — Read Numbers 14

> . . . nations who have heard this report about you will say, "The Lord was not able. . . ." — Num. 14:15

The 1982 SMU Mustangs enjoyed one of their greatest seasons in the school's history. They finished the season ranked second in the nation largely because of the unselfishness of two outstanding running backs. Eric Dickerson and Craig James would have been Heisman Trophy candidates if they had not shared the position. Together they became the NCAA's most potent duo, rushing for a record 8,129 yards. SMU's Pony Express tandem thought first of team success and put personal advancement behind.

As leader of a great nation, Moses is in a predicament in Numbers 14. The faithless Israelites, believing a bad report about their destiny, formed a Back Immediately to Egypt (BITE) Committee and began complaining against their miracle-working God. The Lord had heard enough and was set to destroy them all when Moses, thinking of God's reputation among the heathen, intercedes on behalf of his people. Putting self-advancement behind him (God offered to start a new nation with Moses), Moses prayed that God would spare Israel for the glory of God, whose reputation for great miracles had spread far and wide. Moses knew that the pagan nations would twist God's actions and spread lies about the Lord and His power, so he asked God to spare Israel from immediate annihilation. The Lord heard and answered Moses' prayer, though he chastised the nation severely by refusing the dissenters entrance into the Promised Land.

What about us? Are we jealous for the glory of God and His reputation? God deserves the esteem of others, but sometimes we are more concerned for what is said of us than of Him. Our attitudes should be: "He must become greater; I must become less" (John 3:30).

Consider: *How can you let Jesus become greater in your life?*

A Tarnished Reputation

Moses   Read Numbers 20:1–13

"Because you did not trust in me enough to honor me as holy in the sight of the Israelites. . . ."   Num. 20:12

Many great opportunities have been lost and careers tainted by an impulsive display of anger or frustration. At the conclusion of the 1978 Gator Bowl, Woody Hayes, one of the best college coaches of all time, expressed his frustration by punching a Clemson player who had intercepted a pass on a final Ohio State drive that could have won the game for OSU. His career was ended, and his reputation tarnished by that one impulsive response.

Moses experienced frustration and reacted similarly while leading Israel through the desert. Though God had provided miraculously during forty years of wandering, the Israelites complained at Kadesh because they had no water. Their griping upset Moses, and he responded by going to the Lord for direction. God told him to take his staff and speak to a rock, then water would come forth for the people (v. 8).

After gathering the people together, Moses' disgust and frustration got the best of him, and rather than give God the glory, he stole it for himself. "Must *we* bring you water out of this rock?" he asked as he struck the rock twice in disobedience. Though God still faithfully provided for His people, Moses' anger cost him dearly. He was not allowed the satisfaction of entering Canaan with the nation he had led through the desert for forty years. How costly his loss of composure for one moment!

Sometimes, the best of God's men do not trust Him as they ought. Through Moses' life, we see the consequences of not following God's instructions exactly, of usurping some of His glory for ourselves, and of venting anger and frustration. The antidote for anger is trust in God. So much more blessing and reward Moses would have had if he had remained calm in adverse circumstances.

Consider: *How do you act when you are frustrated or angry?*

Dwelling on the Positive

Joshua   Read Joshua 1:1–18

"I will give you every place where you set your foot, as I promised Moses."
Josh. 1:3

The miracle Mets of 1969, cellar-dwellers in 1968, made a great turnaround under Manager Gil Hodges as they beat Baltimore in the World Series in five games. Hodges's heart attack the year before had much to do with the turnaround. As Gil recovered, he determined to stress to his players the fundamentals of the game and the proper attitude toward defeat. As he put it, "You tend to become what you think about."

Joshua 1 contains some of the most positive inspiration from God that anyone has ever heard. After forty years of desert wandering, the military commander Joshua is to lead his nation into Canaan. Although facing superior forces, Joshua did not dwell on his own weakness but listened to God's words of instruction and promise: "I will give you every place where you set your foot" (v. 3). "No one will be able to stand up against you" (v. 5). "Be strong and courageous . . ." (vv. 6–7).

God promised to be with Joshua as He had been with Moses (v. 5). To keep up his courage, Joshua was to meditate day and night on God's law (v. 8). In so doing, he was guaranteed success. Therefore, Joshua boldly gave the command to move out (v. 10). He had learned that in finding out God is all we have, we realize He is all we need.

What is your attitude toward God and His marching orders? Do you really believe He is going before you in every detail? If you are meditating on His Word and obeying His voice, He promises you success in the things that really count in life. Good relationships with others, a positive witness for Christ, and fulfillment in life will result as you rest in God and His promises.

Consider: *What promises of God are you living on?*

Never Too Bad to Be Saved

Rahab   Read Joshua 2

". . . the Lord your God is God in heaven above and on the earth below."
Josh. 2:11

Before becoming a Christian, Detroit Tigers catcher John Wockenfuss was called Wild Man because of his reactions to failure on the field. He would throw bats, cuss, and punch holes in the dugout. "It was really no way to act," says John, "but since accepting Christ into my life, He's enabled me to deal with this. Instead of all of the pressure being on my shoulders, He's put it on His shoulders. Now when the game is over, it's over. And you know, I just praise the Lord that I made it through without injuries." What a change Christ makes in a life! John Wockenfuss was not too bad to be saved. Christ died for those whose social conduct is unacceptable, as well as for those whose conduct is acceptable.

Consider Rahab in Joshua 2. Although a prostitute, she was the only recorded person in Jericho who expressed faith in the God of Israel. By her saving faith, she welcomed spies into the city (Heb. 11:31) and hid them from the soldiers. Though God did not commend her lie that sent the king's men out of the city as the two spies escaped, He did commend Rahab's faith and motives. And though God hates prostitution, the Lord used her life in a great way for His glory and for the good of His people. This heroine of faith is still remembered because of her trust in a mighty God.

No matter what you've done, God will redeem and use you if you'll hang the scarlet cord (a symbol of Christ's blood spilled on the cross) in the window of your heart. No one is too bad to be saved and no one is so good he doesn't need to be saved!

Consider: *What's the difference between a bad sinner and a good sinner?*

The Right Person for the Job

Joshua   Read Joshua 5:13—6:27

". . . but as commander of the army of the Lord I have now come."
Josh. 5:14

Joe Altobelli, in his first year as manager of the Baltimore Orioles, proved to be just what the O's needed in 1983. "I was in awe of the man," said catcher Rick Dempsey. "Joe is intelligent enough to know that he doesn't have to yell at us or kick us." Dempsey, in response to Altobelli's leadership, hit .385 in the World Series and was named Series Co-MVP when Baltimore captured the championship.

Someone else was just the right person for Joshua and the Israelites as they entered Canaan. The Israelite commander was contemplating how and when to attack the first city in their path. Possibly he sat on a hill outside the city and calculated how many battering rams, weapons, and men would be required. He may have been in prayer. Suddenly, the Commander of the Lord's army appeared before him. No one other than Jesus Christ Himself would have accepted, even directed, the worship of His servant Joshua! Christ is always just the one we need! The Lord told Joshua that He had an overall heavenly purpose for Israel in the coming conflict. Even though God's instructions for conquering Jericho seemed strange, Joshua followed them to the letter, and overwhelming victory was won.

What is your need today? In loneliness, are you in need of a companion? In fear, are you in need of boldness? In impatience, are you in need of rest? Jesus is just the one to meet every need of the human heart. He promises to supply all your needs according to His glorious riches (Phil. 4:19). What a wonderful Savior!

Consider: *What needs can you bring for Christ to fulfill?*

Bitter or Better?

Caleb   ·   Read Joshua 14:6–15

"Now give me this hill country that the Lord promised me that day."
Josh. 14:12

Every so often the endurance of one of sports elder statesmen captures the imagination and inspires the youthfulness and creativity of the over-forty generation. Such was the case with George Blanda in the early seventies when the ageless kicker set numerous records playing for the Oakland Raiders. Baseball's Satchel Paige ("Never look back; something may be gaining on you") did the same in his day, and 1983 saw aging Pete Rose continue his hustle and daring while performing for the Philadelphia Phillies.

Caleb had a similar spirit in his old age. His goal had been to serve the Lord wholeheartedly. As one of the twelve spies Moses had sent to inspect Canaan forty years earlier, only he and Joshua had enough faith to advise Israel to conquer it in the name of Jehovah. For his faith, which had persisted during the forty years of wandering in the desert, Moses had promised him the hill country of Hebron. Now that the Israelites were in the land, as an eighty-five-year-old man, Caleb boldly claims it as his to conquer and settle. Caleb's faith and his fitness are just as strong in his old age as in the prime of his manhood. He trusts God just as he did earlier.

It has been said that the circumstances of life can make us bitter or better. The difference is our reaction. Everyone knows elderly people whose countenance expresses great faith in God. We may know others who have become cynical or depressed about life. We cannot control our circumstances as we grow older, but we can control our responses to them. What will the next generation say about you? Will your life inspire others to attempt great things for God as Caleb's did?

Consider: *Are life's circumstances serving to make you bitter or better?*

Dare to Be Different

Again the Israelites cried out to the Lord, and he gave them a deliverer—
Ehud, a left-handed man. . . .   Judg. 3:15

One of college football's most inspiring performances occurred October 4, 1969 on national television. Red-haired, freckled
Archie Manning of Ole Miss led his Rebels up and down the field
against Alabama, passing for 436 yards and running for 104 in a
heartbreaking 33-32 loss to the Crimson Tide. The sideline camera
shot of Archie's tears washing his muddy face clean in the last
seconds captured the hearts of millions of fans. Though Archie went
on to become All-Pro and an MVP in the NFL, he always seemed to
stand out as the lone star on a losing team.

Ehud was another aggressive redhead who had to stand
alone against overwhelming circumstances. Not only was he red-
headed (Ehud means "red hair"), but he was a southpaw in a world
of right-handers. He seemed, however, to be the only one with
enough courage to trust God to deliver Israel from bondage to the
Moabites. Actually, God had raised up this judge of Israel for this
very purpose. By faith, he put his life on the line and led the
overthrow of wicked King Eglon, leading to eighty years of peace in
Israel. He didn't let being different or standing alone deter him from
achieving great things for God.

What is your unique ability, characteristic, or talent? God has
given you a means of glorifying Him in a way no one else can. Are
you content with His designed plan for you? In trying to be like
everyone else, are you letting others press you into a mold that robs
God of the glory He desires from your life?

Consider: *How can you serve God uniquely?*

Score One for the Common Man

Shamgar . . . struck down six hundred Philistines with an oxgoad.

Judg. 3:31

Often a simple tool that is *available* is used to accomplish great things. *Spotlight* reports that Dr. James Naismith, a pastor, left his church to work with the YMCA because he felt he could do more good working with young people. While using two peach baskets as goals for his new game, he initiated basketball. Years later, Naismith's daughter heard a Christian athlete share of his travels overseas to witness "with a basketball in one hand and a Bible in the other." She responded, "My father would be so pleased if he knew that basketball was being used for some purpose other than just to make a few people rich."

God used a common man with a common tool to deliver His people from slavery to the Philistines. Shamgar was the son of Anath (a pagan god of sex and war) and evidently not a believer in God. The peasant family of Shamgar had only an oxgoad (an eight-foot wooden rod used to herd oxen) with which to fight, since the conquering Philistines allowed them no iron weapons or tools. Yet, God blessed the faith of Shamgar and because he was available and willing, took what he had and used it to save the people.

Our God can carry out His purpose in this world despite apparent disadvantages. He doesn't require a great man as the world considers greatness. Notice that Shamgar did not even come from a family of faith in God. Still, he trusted the Lord, gave what he had, and God delivered an entire nation through him.

Consider: *What has God given you to glorify Him with?*

Keep the Wind and Rain Behind You

Deborah   Read Judges 4

Then Deborah said to Barak, "Go! This is the day the Lord has given Sisera
into your hands."   Judg. 4:14

Diversity devastates some people; others' responses cause
them to rise higher. Rafer Johnson, though born with a clubfoot,
became one of the greatest decathalon champions. Pro-football
kicker Tom Dempsey holds the record for the longest NFL field
goal, despite having only half a foot on his kicking leg. Miler Glenn
Cunningham, severely burned in a fire, became a champion on the
cinders.

According to the Jewish historian Josephus, God once used
adverse elements to help His people in the destruction of their
enemies. Because of sin, Israel again had been subjected to
slavery (4:1). After twenty years, they cried out to God in repentance
(4:3), and He sent the prophetess Deborah, a political and spiritual
leader, and the military leader Barak to deliver them. Though
heavily outnumbered (Jabin had 300,000 footmen, 10,000 horse-
men and 3,000 chariots), God supernaturally gave Israel great
victory. Josephus records that when the battle began, a large
quantity of rain, hail, and wind came into the face of the Canaanites
but at the backs of the Israelites. Realizing God was with them, they
took great courage and routed their enemy.

God allows storms in the lives of His children, as well as in
the lives of the unsaved. The difference is that He sends them to
help believers conform to the image of Christ (Rom. 8:29). To the
nonbeliever, God often sends adversity to turn him to Christ.

Consider: *What storm of life has aided you?*

Weak Enough to Win

Gideon   Read Judges 6:1–24

"But Lord, how can I save Israel? My clan is the weakest . . . and I am the least. . . ."   Judg. 6:15

Often it is not the best player who becomes the best coach of an athletic team. The guy who hustles for everything while playing the game learns things that more talented players may not discover. Not many superstars have made good coaches in professional baseball; yet, many second stringers or minor-league players have become great managers.

Gideon was a second stringer during times of great fear in Israel. Once more, sin had resulted in God's judgment, and foreign powers raided the land at every harvest. Finally, Israel repented (v. 6), and God worked in their behalf.

First, God selected a man who would trust Him—not a man who had great ability, but a coward who was hiding his wheat in a winepress. Certainly, no one but the Lord would receive glory for the deliverance! In calling him, the angel of God (Jesus Christ) saw Gideon not as he was, but as he could be. He addressed Gideon as "mighty warrior" (v. 12). Though physically strong (Gideon means "hewer"), evidently he was unsure of himself and suffered from an inferiority complex, since he questioned God about his assignment. But Gideon had an awe and respect for God (v. 22). That's what God was looking for.

What about you? Did you fail to make the all-star team? No matter. God can and will use you anyway. In fact, He delights to do it this way. All He's looking for is willingness and an appreciation of His power.

Consider: *Why does God use us in our weakness?*

The Stiffest Test

. . . because he was afraid of his family and the men of the town, he did it at
night. . . .   Judg. 6:27

Through the encouragement of Giant pitcher Al Worthington,
rookie outfielder Felipe Alou received Jesus Christ as his personal
Savior in June of 1958. Later, he decided to leave his family's
church, a massive organization that dominated his native Domini-
can Republic. Friends and family rejected and criticized him. In *My
Life and Baseball,* Felipe recalls how little he had heard about
Jesus Christ during his childhood and how much Mary had been
worshiped. Clarifying that he didn't hate his family, he recalled that
when Christ came into his life, he hungered for God's Word, which
was not taught and even opposed for the common man by his
family's church leaders. Certainly, it was difficult for Felipe Alou to
follow Christ in his own hometown.

Gideon had to take a similar stand when he truly met God. In
obedience to the Lord's directions, he destroyed his father's altar to
the pagan god Baal as well as the symbols of the false gods of his
people at night because of his fear of the society in which he grew
up. Scripture says that he had reason to fear, since the men of the
town wanted to kill him. Because of Gideon's obedience, however,
his father had a change of heart and quieted the mob.

Sometimes God asks us as Christians to take a stand, maybe
against our own family's beliefs. Jesus said, "Anyone who loves his
father or mother more than me is not worthy of me; and anyone who
loves his son or daughter more than me is not worthy of me" (Matt.
10:37). But He also talks about the reward of such a stand (Mark
10:29—30). Probably the most difficult place to confess Christ is at
home before your own family. Yet, it is better to be honored by the
Lord than to be esteemed by men.

Consider: *Have you shared Jesus with your family?*

Decide Who Will Guide

Gideon   Read Judges 6:36−40

If you will save Israel . . . as you have promised.   Judg. 6:36

A father delights in an obedient son, just as a coach delights in a submissive player. When father is coach and son is player, the situation is even more unique. Such a situation occurred for San Jose State Coach Jack Elway and Sanford quarterback John Elway in the 1983 East-West Shrine Football Game. For two weeks, the media proclaimed, "See Heisman Trophy candidate John Elway— coached by his father." Certainly, Coach Elway left no doubt about his will for his son in leading the West squad that day. Yet, John had the freedom and responsibility to make some decisions that had to be made on the field. Following the guidance of his father, John won the Offensive Player of the Game Award.

Gideon was indecisive in following the will of God. Though the Lord had plainly said He wanted Gideon to deliver Israel from Midian (6:14) and had given him the power to do it (6:34), when it came time, Gideon questioned God. His lack of faith led him to ask twice for a physical sign.

How can we know God's will for our lives? God wants us to study His Word—where most of His will is already revealed—not depend on physical signs. His plan includes our salvation, a holy lifestyle, and that we share Christ with others, study Scripture, pray, and fellowship with other believers. Beyond this, He wants us to do everything to His glory (1 Cor. 1:31). He sends His peace to act as an umpire in our hearts for areas not covered in Scripture (Col. 3:15). Then, we must decide and trust God for the results. Once we decide to glorify Him in everything, the biggest hurdle is cleared.

Are you uncertain of God's will? After prayer, Bible study, and consulting mature Christian counsel, make the decision you feel is right and believe that He is giving guidance (Prov. 3:5−6).

Consider: *How do you make decisions?*

Out of Control

"Remember, I am your flesh. . . ."   Judg. 9:2

Former major-league manager Al Dark is known as a faithful Christian who practices what he preaches. But in the midst of his San Francisco Giants' sixth straight loss in 1961, he verbally attacked Umpire Shag Crawford and was ejected from the game. The San Francisco *Examiner* quoted him the next day as saying, "My wife, Adrienne, says I should be ashamed of myself and I thoroughly agree. It wasn't a Christian thing to do. It was Satan's work. Never before have I so addressed any man—and with the Lord's help, I hope to have the strength never to do so again."

We must respect Al Dark for honestly confessing that his fleshly nature had momentarily taken control of his actions. Even the most devout believers are not immune to the old nature's subtle attacks. The Old Testament story of Abimelech (a symbol of the flesh) describes what happens when an antihero gains control. When Gideon died, the Israelites returned to their idolatry (v. 33). They forgot God and Gideon (vv. 34—35). Gideon had seventy sons who could have ruled the nation. But one son, Abimelech, grew power hungry and caused a rebellion in which his sixty-nine brothers were brutally murdered. Abimelech represents our old sin nature. No matter how spiritual we think ourselves to be, our tendency to sin is there waiting to damage the cause of Christ and ourselves. Abimelech was ungrateful, rebellious, selfishly ambitious, a murderer of his own brothers, without conscience, and jealous for his reputation. (See Gal. 5:19—21.)

With flesh in control, civil war takes place. Only by reckoning the flesh dead and yielding to God's Spirit (Rom. 6) can we please Him.

Consider: *Which nature is controlling you?*

A Victim of Discrimination

                                Read Judges 11:1–11

So Jepthah fled from his brothers and settled in the land of Tob. . . .
Judg. 11:3

From 1898 to 1946, blacks were barred from organized baseball by a gentleman's agreement. They played in the Negro leagues, which developed into an American institution. Willie Mays, Hank Aaron, Ernie Banks, Elston Howard, Jim Gillian, and other stars all came from the black leagues after Branch Rickey of the Dodgers signed Jackie Robinson in 1945. Other great players who were past their prime or out of baseball when the color line was broken never received the acclaim they might have received in the American or National leagues. Fortunately in 1971, Commissioner Bowie Kuhn formed a committee with power to elect them to the Hall of Fame, and many Negro league stars did receive the long overdue recognition they deserved.

Jepthah of Gilead was also discriminated against, even by his own family. Driven out of the house, he became a leader of a wandering army. There was something special about Jepthah, however. Amid the idolatry of the Israelites, he knew God. He referred to Jehovah ("the covenant-keeping God") more than any other leader in Judges. Though immature, he was committed. Though shallow in his knowledge of God, he knew God was real. Though the son of a harlot, he was born again. In God's time, the door opened for Jepthah to deliver Israel from oppression. He was promised the leadership of Gilead if he would deliver them. Notice the response: He prayed about it first (v. 11), accepted the challenge, and a great deliverance followed (vv. 32–33).

Are you rejected by some group or individual? Maybe opportunity seems to pass you by. Society may turn us away, but God never will. Get to know Him intimately, and when opportunity does come, He will help you make the most of it.

Consider: *How do you handle rejection?*

Know Where You're Going

Jepthah   Read Judges 11:28—40

"Whatever comes out of the door of my house . . . I will sacrifice. . . ."
Judg: 11:31

Atlanta Braves right-hander Pascual Perez received national attention and the nickname I-285 when he got lost driving to Atlanta's Fulton County Stadium in 1982. Heading for a scheduled start during the pennant race, he circled Atlanta for hours. He finally arrived at the stadium after the game had begun, missing his starting assignment.

While losing one's bearings on the highway can hurt, spiritual ignorance and misdirection can be devastating. Though Jepthah was God's man and his heart was right before God, he made a foolish vow to God in an attempt to insure victory in battle. "You give me the Ammonites and I'll give you a burnt offering of whoever and whatever greets me first upon returning home," he said. Probably he thought a slave would be first to greet him. He tried to pay for God's favor instead of resting in His grace because in his weak faith, he was afraid God would abandon him halfway through the battle.

With great agony, he saw his only child first greet him. His foolish vow now became a trap, and he ignorantly followed through on his rash promise. He didn't even stop to search Scripture or consult his spiritual leaders. If he had, he would have discovered that God prohibits human sacrifice (Deut. 12:31, 18:10) and he could have redeemed his daughter and saved her (Lev. 27).

Enthusiasm without knowledge is deadly. What Jepthah didn't know cost him dearly. It wasn't enough to have a heart to please God; he needed the *knowledge* of the Lord. God's people are destroyed for lack of knowledge (Hos. 4:6). The way to gain knowledge of Him is to study His Word. We cannot afford ignorance.

Consider: *Have you studied God's Word today?*

Unlimited Potential

Samson   Read Judges 13

He grew and the Lord blessed him, and the Spirit of the Lord began to stir
him. . . .   Judg. 13:24–25

As Hershal Walker ran his way into the record books for three
years at the University of Georgia, his potential to become one of
the greatest players of all time became apparent. His size, speed,
and savvy on the field made him stand out. But Hershal's first
season with the New Jersey Generals didn't bring him the fame he
had enjoyed at Georgia. His potential had yet to be realized.

Samson was another strong man who was blessed with
unlimited potential. God had his life mapped out for him from birth.
Like the births of Isaac, Samuel, and the Lord Jesus, Samson's was
extraordinary. Probably the greatest opportunity ever presented a
man was given to Samson when God said that he would begin to
deliver Israel (v. 5). For his part, Samson was to walk with God,
preferring God's company. He was to drink no wine (a symbol of
earthly merrymaking) in an area famous for choice wines, have no
haircuts (a public witness to others of God's presence), and never
go near a dead body (which would have made him ceremonially
unfit for temple service). As a result of Samson's faith, God used
him to do great things. He became known as the strongest man who
ever lived because his strength came from God.

The same resource available to Samson is ours today. God's
same Holy Spirit indwells all believers and stirs us, as we allow
Him. His supernatural power enables us to overcome all obstacles
and to accomplish God's will. We have unlimited potential to
become all God wants us to be! By faith, we must recognize this
power and allow God to manifest Himself through us. This means
preferring God first, becoming bold in our witness, and shunning
sin.

Consider: *How much of your potential in Christ have you realized?*

Conquered by Overconfidence

Samson went down to Timnah and saw there a young Philistine woman.
Judg. 14:1

Overconfidence has gotten more than one athlete in deep trouble. Raider cornerback James Davis intercepted a Denver pass during the 1982 season and raised his hands overhead to celebrate at the 20-yard line. He was hit from behind by a hustling Bronco! In 1971 when Steeler tightend David Smith waved the ball short of the goal, it slipped away and bounced through the end zone for a touchback! Steeler coach Chuck Noll wasn't very happy, especially since his club lost 38-16 to Kansas City that night. He fined Smith two hundred dollars!

Things looked good for Samson, too, until he became overconfident and went to the enemy of Timnah. Although God had commanded him to abstain from intermarriage with the idol worshipers of Canaan (Deut. 7:1–4), Samson saw a woman he wanted for his wife. God allowed Samson to have her, but Samson paid dearly, suffering every time he went into Philistine territory. His marriage to this Philistine woman began his downward spiral. What happened to God's Incredible Hulk who had so much promise? He had all the externals right—no haircut, no wine, no contact with the dead. But he neglected a consistent walk with God, so the deep internal love of God and trust in Him was missing. As his appetites became more powerful than his vow, overconfidence got the best of him.

Is overconfidence setting you up for a fall? If so, stop trusting in your own power, position, prestige, or perfection to get things done and trust God by faith. He can do more with His little finger in an instant than you can do with the effort of a lifetime! In ourselves we are weak, but in Christ we are made strong (2 Cor. 12:9). God-confidence is better than self-confidence!

Consider: *Why is self-reliance a sin?*

The Power of Negative Thinking

Samson   Read Judges 15

They said to him, "We've come to tie you up and hand you over to the Philistines."   Judg. 15:12

Game seven of the 1958 World Series between the Yankees and the Braves is a classic example of the power of thought life. The game was deadlocked 3-3 in the last of the ninth when the Yankees' Elston Howard stepped to the plate against the Braves' left-hander Warren Spahn. At a conference on the mound, Spahn was reminded *again* not to throw a fast ball high and away from Howard, whose favorite pitch was high and away. Where do you think the next pitch was? That's right, high and away! Howard hit it out of the park to win the game and the World Series. Spahn said later that he knew Howard's strength, but the *constant* thought about it subconsciously led him to throw the ball there!

Judges 15 tells the story of what was probably Samson's finest hour. Pursued by the evil Philistines and sold out by his own nation, Samson alone was used by God to begin to deliver Israel. Samson retained the passion for freedom that his people had lost. His was no apathetic attitude at a time when his nation had accepted the status quo and even turned against him. Like the Lord Jesus, he willingly offered himself for the nation. Then God's Spirit came upon him in power (v. 14). He burst through the ropes, picked up a donkey's jawbone, and killed one thousand of the enemy single-handedly. Then this hero of faith gained the allegiance of Israel and led them for twenty years (v. 20).

People who are lukewarm toward God usually persecute those who want to trust Him. Throughout history, religious people (those with outward form) have been the greatest hindrance to those committed to Jesus Christ. Satan loses no sleep over those who give God lip service, but he is awfully busy trying to use them to discourage those who give God life service.

Consider: *How is negative thinking hurting you today?*

The Importance of Influence

Samson   Read Judges 16:1−21

So he told her everything.   Judg. 16:17

Superstar Mike Schmidt of the Philadelphia Phillies strives to set a good example for others to follow. "I could be a drinker and a hell-raiser," he says, "but it's important to me that I'm not. I won't go places where you'll see me talking with a bunch of women. I think of it this way: If a kid has a Mike Schmidt poster in his bedroom, I'd want his parents to be happy about it."

Mike Schmidt takes his influence seriously and seeks to protect it. In contrast, after twenty years of ruling Israel, Samson grew careless about his influence and his position. He went to the enemy city of Gaza, where he visited a prostitute and had a narrow escape. Then he met Delilah in the Valley of Sorek. He loved her and grew loyal to her. In return, she used him and sold him to his enemies. But her task wasn't easy. On three separate occasions Samson toyed with her, alluding to the secret of his supernatural strength but never telling the secret. The longer he played with fire, the closer he came to being burned. Eventually it happened. Her nagging and prodding finally wore him down (v. 16). When he told her everything, he lost his hair, the power of God, his eyes, his influence, and finally his freedom.

God is gracious when He saves us, gives us His Spirit, blesses us with influence, and trusts us with physical and spiritual strength. To take these things lightly is to court disaster.

Satan has temptations set for us in our areas of weakness. For Samson, it was Delilah. He could have escaped if he had remembered his influence and fled the scene (2 Tim. 2:22). But he played the fool, and his life was never the same again.

Consider: *How are you careless about your influence?*

43

The Comeback

Samson   Read Judges 16:22–31

But the hair on his head began to grow again after it had been shaved.
Judg. 16:22

Football history's most celebrated mistake took place in the 1929 Georgia Tech-California Rose Bowl Game when California's Roy Riegals picked up a loose ball and ran toward the wrong goal. A teammate finally tackled the befuddled Riegals on his own one-yard line. Though disconsolate, Riegals came back to play a great second half and the next year captained California to a big year. He was a man who made a mistake but didn't stay defeated.

In spite of all his mistakes, Samson ended life in victory. Grinding blindly day after day in prison was a tremendous defeat for the Israelite hero. But verse 22 is one of the most encouraging verses in the Bible because it implies that as he labored, his faith began to grow, along with his hair. This hulk of a man remembered his God, and gradually the power of God returned. The opportunity to fulfill his destiny was yet to come.

During an orgy in honor of their god Dagon, a great crowd of Philistines sent for Samson to entertain them. Familiar with his surroundings, Samson asked to rest against the columns support-ing the bleachers that held three thousand Philistines. Praying one last time for the God of Israel to strengthen him, he collapsed the structure upon himself and his enemies. Samson had failed in many ways, but a sovereign God used him to accomplish His purpose. The Philistine power was broken.

Ever blown it really big? God's grace for Samson should encourage you. Though He disciplined Samson severely, God finished the maturing and refining process and used him once again.

Consider: *Can God give you strength to start over?*

Refusing to Compromise

"May the Lord repay you for what you have done."   Ruth 2:12

In an age when winning is all that counts to many people, Detroit Tiger owner Tom Monaghan made a refreshing statement. In the November 14, 1983 issue of *Sporting News* Monaghan was quoted as saying he would not "compromise my values to win." This comment reveals true character. What an athletic world we would have if all owners and players had that attitude!

Boaz also placed a high premium on positive character traits in himself and in others. Though he was a rich land owner in charge of many servants, he showed consideration for a lowly servant girl named Ruth. Then he followed Hebrew law to the letter in acquiring her hand in marriage. To provide stability for the land, the law provided that the nearest relative of a deceased man take his wife and raise sons, so the dead man's family might not cease. Even though another man was first in line for Ruth, he declined for economic reasons. Therefore, Boaz was able to "redeem" Ruth and continue the family line. His son Obed became father of Jesse, who became father of David. David, a man after God's own heart, became king of Israel and an ancestor of Joseph, the earthly provider for the Lord Jesus during His early years. This heritage of positive character traits was of great value in future generations.

How much do you value moral character? Is it important in your life and in the lives of your friends? Is it more important to you to become like Jesus (Rom. 8:29) than to win ball games, acquire wealth, or gain prestige? Is the approval of God more valuable to you than the praise of men? Or are you more interested in obtaining material and sensual gratification? Like Boaz, you will be repaid according to your deeds of character.

Consider: *How often do you compromise to win?*

A Call to the Major League

Then the Lord called Samuel.   1 Sam. 3:4

Minor-league ballplayers live daily in hopes of receiving a call to report to the next higher league. Every manager files a daily report on how the players performed, and each athlete reviews his performance mentally and emotionally, wondering how it has affected his chances to move up. Every hit, run, strike out, or walk affects to some degree the club's judgment of the player and the player's hope for a call.

In 1 Samuel 3, God called the boy Samuel to give His Word to Israel. Though divine appearances and messages were rare (v. 1), God saw fit to raise and use a young man who had honored Him in his life (1 Sam. 20:26, 30). Though the call was plain, Samuel didn't discern it at first. Once he realized who was calling him, Samuel answered obediently. He became a mouthpiece for God; none of his words were wasted (v. 19).

God wants to do something special in each of our lives, too. But we really don't believe it is He who is calling us. Maybe we'd know what He's saying more often if we spent less time doing things and more time listening to Him speak through His Word. Time spent *with* Him alone is an indication of our love *for* Him. Jesus' purpose in calling His disciples was first of all that they might be *with* Him (Mark 3:14). Only then is He able to communicate to us.

How about you? Do you believe God will call you to serve Him? Will you spend more time with Him, so He can use you in a greater way? Someone has said, "You'll never be anything for God in public until you spend time with Him in private." Go alone to a quiet place with His Word and ask Him to gently communicate His plan to you. Do not be in a hurry. God will give you wondrous guidance and peace in His presence.

Consider: *Why did God speak to Samuel and not to Eli?*

A Majority of One

Jonathan   Read 1 Samuel 14

"Nothing can hinder the Lord from saving, whether by many or by few."
1 Sam. 14:6

The 1980 Olympic Games are best remembered in this country by the miracle hockey upset of the powerful Russians by American college players. After the final horn, our underdog squad erupted with uncontrolled elation on the ice. Before the game, the USA coach had challenged our players, calling it the "moment you were born for." An intense contest ensued, and *Sports Illustrated* captured a tremendous cover photo of the celebration. Millions of Americans who had never seen a hockey game became patriotic overnight. Nothing sparks the spirit like an underdog succeeding!

No underdog in Scripture stands taller as a hero than Jonathan in 1 Samuel 14. When everything in Israel's army was falling apart—widespread fear, mass desertion, and inferior weapons—Jonathan decided to trust God. Faith led him to take action. He not only believed that God plus one made a majority but also an advantage. Therefore, he attempted a task so large that if God had not been involved, the project would have failed and probably cost him his life.

What happened? With a servant, he killed twenty Philistines, and the rest panicked when God sent an earthquake. The enemy turned on each other in ignorance. Saul's army was revived as men returned to the ranks and took up the chase of the enemy. God gave Jonathan a great victory.

Have you insurmountable odds against you today? Thank God for them and allow Him to direct you. Then, don't hesitate to step out by faith and attempt great things for God. When the Lord wants to accomplish something, the faith of one man is unbeatable. He will surely use you to glorify His name.

Consider: *Is your God bigger than circumstances?*

The Price of Breaking the Rules

Saul   Read 1 Samuel 15

"To obey is better than sacrifice. . . ."   1 Sam. 15:22

Driver Richard Petty, the biggest name in racing, was disciplined during the summer of 1983 in one of NASCAR's greatest controversies. It was discovered that Petty used illegal tires and an oversized engine for a five-hundred-mile race in Charlotte, S.C. He was fined a NASCAR record of thirty-five thousand dollars, his engine was confiscated, and he lost 104 points toward a high finish in the yearly standings. Though some felt the penalty should have been even greater, it was very costly and dishonorable for a driver who was only two wins away from his two-hundredth career victory.

King Saul also discovered how costly disobedience can be. Established by God as Israel's first king, he was commanded to wage a campaign against the pagan Amalekites. God told Saul exactly what to do and why (vv. 2–3)—he was to totally destroy everything in the camp of Amalek.

Saul only partially obeyed. Unfortunately, his materialism and tolerance for evil led him to spare the wicked King Agag and the best animals. When confronted by Samuel, Saul blamed others for his sin (v. 15) and revealed that his fear of men outweighed his respect for God's orders (v. 24). His whole response was one of self-justification. Even after acknowledging his sin Saul was more concerned about his reputation than about turning to God in repentance. Because of his attitude, he lost the kingdom. What a costly and dishonorable penalty!

God still desires obedience from His children. It is more important to listen to Him and respond by faith than it is to make sacrifices to appease Him. Only the sacrifice of Christ on Calvary can please our holy God. Let us rest in His love and obey His voice out of love for Him.

Consider: *Which is easier for you, to obey God or to sacrifice?*

Too Big to Miss

David   Read 1 Samuel 17

"... I come against you in the name of the Lord Almighty. ..."
                                                            1 Sam. 17:45

An outstanding defensive lineman can cause havoc for an offensive football team, especially if he has the mobility to pursue the play. Sometimes, the strategy used against these agile tacklers is to line up and run right at them. Different blocking schemes may be used, but attacking the problem is often more effective than running from it.

Long ago, a shepherd boy named David was serving at the training table for his brothers (v. 17) when he became aware of a nine-and-one-half-foot problem facing his nation. Goliath would have been quite a defensive lineman if he hadn't been preoccupied with taunting and intimidating the people of God. The PFL (Palestinian Football League) must have been counting the days until Goliath would be discharged from the Philistine Army and they could wave a fat contract in front of his wide angle face! His mere presence sent spasms of fear into the hearts of the Israelites; no one challenged him. Everyone thought he was too big to hit—everyone except David. Recounting past victories in the power of God (v. 37) and forsaking natural means of warfare (vv. 38–39), David took a sling and five stones and attacked this overgrown Philistine. Confident in his God, David even told Goliath in advance what was going to happen and why (v. 46). His motive was God's glory. A nine-and-one-half-foot pagan was no contest for a boy trusting God. He was too big to miss!

Got any oversized giants in your life? Take a lesson from David. Making God's glory your motive and forsaking the weapons of the flesh, attack the problem head on, trusting God to deliver you. Once the big giant bites the dust, the many smaller ones will flee the scene.

Consider: *What giant can you trust God to defeat in your life?*

49

Jealous of Success

David   Read 1 Samuel 18

... Saul kept a jealous eye on David.   1 Sam. 18:9

Most athletes probably don't receive all the praise they feel they deserve. In fact, few people will ever receive all the credit and adoration they would like. A problem can develop in a ball club, however, when one or two star players are especially lauded by the public. Human nature being what it is, the chances are great that others will become jealous. Soon, players start comparing themselves with each other, worrying about their own statistics, and generally putting self-interests ahead of team goals. Morale is adversely affected; team play suffers.

David's rapid and early success as a military hero became a real test for King Saul—a test he flunked royally. With Goliath vanquished, David's growing trust in God resulted in greater and greater victories. As the people's praise of their young hero increased, the veteran King Saul grew green with envy. He became angry (v. 8), suspicious (v. 9), and finally tried to murder David (v. 11). After failing, he grew fearful of David (v. 12). It became increasingly obvious that as David trusted God, the Lord blessed him with success in everything he did. But instead of rejoicing that God was blessing one of his loyal subjects (for the good of his nation), Saul allowed a spirit of envy to torment him constantly. His life was consumed by jealousy.

Take a quick attitude check. Do you rejoice in the success of your peers? Are you genuinely happy for their success, even if you must take second place in the opinions of others? If not, jealousy will eat you alive. Sincere love for others will bring you happiness when they succeed. Accept each success of teammates and friends as a test to determine your joy in their achievement. If you fail this test, as Saul did, ask God to take away the bitter spirit of envy and replace it with His love.

Consider: *How much of a team player are you?*

A Loyal Friend

Read 1 Samuel 20

. . . Jonathan became one in spirit with David, and he loved him as himself.
1 Sam. 18:1

When second-baseman Jackie Robinson broke the color line in baseball in 1947, he had to endure boos, thrown objects, and abuse from opposing players as well as some from his own team. One day in Ebbetts Field, he faced an especially difficult trial. As Jackie was tagging a sliding runner, the player raised his spikes and drove them into Robinson's chest. Jackie reacted instantly, and a fight began before the umpires could restore order. Opposing players continued to yell ugly names, however, and fans threw trash at Jackie and howled in rage. Suddenly, shortstop Pee Wee Reese called time-out. He walked over to Robinson as the crowd booed, put his arm around him, and stood beside him in silence. The courageous act of a friend assured Jackie of the support he needed to endure a trying time.

One loyal friend is capable of giving great encouragement, as Jonathan gave David. Both men had trusted God through heroic victories and were drawn together by a common character. In unselfish love, Jonathan gave David prized gifts (18:4) and eagerly helped David when he was unpopular (1 Sam. 20:4). Jonathan even faced death because of his friendship (1 Sam. 20:33). But Jonathan's loyalty is best seen when he helped David find strength in God (1 Sam. 23:16). There's an act of friendship that really helps and endures.

Our friendships tell much about our character. What sort of friendships do you maintain? Do you love only those who are popular? Do you freely and regularly give to help your friends? Can you help someone find strength in God? A lasting friendship requires hard work and may be costly, but it is well worth the time and effort. Commit yourself now to be a better friend.

Consider: *How can you become a better friend?*

Gracious Toward the Enemy

David   Read 1 Samuel 24

"The Lord forbid that I should . . . lift up my hand against him. . . ."
1 Sam. 24:6

According to a story in the *Nashville Tennesseean*, when Coach Frank Kush was at Arizona State, he told Dallas Cowboy Vice President Gil Brandt that he was not welcome on the campus. Kush later moved on to the Baltimore Colts. Just before his season opened, he was in great need of a kicker. Dallas had a good one, in addition to Rafael Septien: Raul Allegre. After hearing of Kush's need, Brandt offered Allegre to the Colts. In four out of five early-season Colt wins, Allegre's kicks provided the winning margin. Brandt later received a letter from Kush, thanking him for his help. What a difference Brandt's kindness to an enemy made!

Like Gil Brandt, David was on the despised list of an influential person. Because of jealousy, King Saul had sworn to kill the young leader. Saul took an army of three thousand men to hunt a man who could not allow himself to hate his enemy. In chapter 24 of 1 Samuel, David proves his love for God and for the man who was hurting him. Given an opportunity to kill his pursuer, David refused, trusting God to deliver him in His time and in His way. Instead of running Saul through with a sword, David meekly cut off a part of Saul's coat as proof to Saul that he meant him no ill. He did this with great humility and respect for Saul's call and position (v. 6). In chapter 26, David again spared Saul's life, setting an example of kindness for all believers.

Has someone recently treated you unfairly or with malice? Resist the tendency to retaliate. Refuse to become bitter (Heb. 12:15). Love and prayer for an enemy has turned many foes into friends. Jesus responded to his enemies by saying, "Father, forgive them. . . ." With His help so can you.

Consider: *Can you compare the end result of kindness with that of retaliation?*

Fallen Hero

But the thing David had done displeased the Lord.   2 Sam. 11:27

Having a morally upright hero is healthy. We need positive role models who show us that great things are indeed possible. Today the reputations of many heroes are tarnished. Well-known sports figures promote alcohol, get busted for cocaine, and reveal a self-centered attitude with unreasonable salary demands. As a result, respect for heroes has declined drastically.

At fifty years of age, David was such a hero. Though a man "after God's own heart," he fell into sin. Notice the sequence of temptation: First, neglecting his business, he sent Joab to lead the army while he stayed home; second, he let his eyes feast and his mind dwell on a beautiful woman; third, he succumbed to his desires, sent for her, and slept with her.

When Bathsheba announced she was pregnant, David compounded his sin by trying to hide it. He made Uriah, her husband, drunk, and finally had him murdered. All this by a man who knew and loved God!

For about a year, David harbored his sin. He suffered mentally and emotionally during this time (Ps. 32:3–4). Then Nathan the prophet confronted David, and David confessed to God (2 Sam. 12). Our gracious God forgave him instantly and restored his joy (Ps. 51). Yet, though the guilt of sin was gone, the consequences and scars of sin remained (2 Sam. 12:13).

Those who are high and mighty have so far to fall. Learn from David and the New Testament, ". . . if you think you're standing firm, be careful that you don't fall!" (1 Cor. 10:12). Expect temptation. Then flee from it! If you have fallen, confess it; it's the only way to regain the joy of your salvation.

Consider: *What do you do to escape temptation?*

Costly Sacrifice

David   Read 2 Samuel 24

"I will not sacrifice to the Lord my God burnt offerings that cost me nothing."
2 Sam. 24:24

One of the most difficult plays in basketball occurs when a defensive player stands his ground near the basket and takes the charge of a driving opponent. Stationary against a determined dribbler, the defender knows he will be run over, yet he must maintain good position and draw the foul for the good of his team. It's a sacrifice that is painful and may even cause injury; yet it demonstrates a team-centered attitude.

King David, a great hero of faith, occasionally sank miserably into unbelief. Some Bible authorities feel his numbering of Israel's armies was his worst sin because he became proud of his own strength and didn't trust God. Even Joab, his army commander, was aware of David's vanity (v. 3).

Sin always brings punishment, and God dealt with David's pride through the death of some seventy thousand people. In agony of soul, David repented and prayed for the end of the slaughter.

Because God accepted David's prayer for forgiveness, He told David to build an altar for sacrifice. Though Araunah offered his threshing floor, wood, and oxen free of charge, David insisted on paying for them. To offer to his Lord something that did not cost was meaningless to David and to God.

What about you? Do you give God your leftover talent, time, and energy, while keeping the best for yourself? Or, do you give Him the strength of your youth, the best of your abilities, the first part of all that comes to you? He is interested in proof of your love by the offering of your best. It's that which costs the giver that is blessed by the Lord.

Consider: *What sacrifice to God have you made that cost you something?*

Wisdom to Rule

"Give your servant a discerning heart to govern your people and to distinguish between right and wrong."   1 Kings 3:9

The summer of 1983 presented American League President Lee MacPhail with one of the most confounding decisions a baseball administrator ever faced. On July 24 in Yankee Stadium, George Brett of the Royals hit a ninth-inning home run to give Kansas City the lead. Yankee manager Billy Martin argued that the homer shouldn't count because Brett's bat had pine tar extending up the handle more than the allowable eighteen inches. The umpires agreed and declared New York victorious. After days of debate, MacPhail overruled the umps and ordered the game completed. He felt that the intent of the rule was to keep balls clean and that violation did not require an "out" call. The Royals eventually won.

A situation like this requires the wisdom that God once gave to King Solomon. Though he had many flaws, Solomon loved God and basically kept the statutes of his father David (v. 3). Power could have given him occasion to sin, but because he had his priorities right, he asked God for wisdom to rule, and the Lord gave him much more than wisdom. "Moreover, I will give you what you have not asked for, both riches and honor—so that in your lifetime you will have no equal among kings" (1 Kings 3:13).

Our omnipotent God gave Solomon both riches and honor because of his humble heart. He also promised Solomon a long life if he continued an obedient walk with God, as David had walked with God (v. 14).

The nature of God is to give exceeding abundance above all we ask or think (Eph. 3:20). But He desires our affections so much, sometimes He withholds material blessings to turn us to Himself. Only when we seek first His kingdom can we claim His blessing.

Consider: *If you could have anything, what would you ask of God?*

Deadly Indecision

Elijah   Read 1 Kings 18

"How long will you waver between two opinions?"   1 Kings 18:21

When a player, coach, or official fails to act decisively, it causes frustration. Years ago in a youth-league baseball game umpired by an inexperienced parent, there was bang-bang tag play at home plate. While the dust cleared, the umpire stood silently as both teams demanded, "Safe or out?" He hesitantly replied, "It's too close to tell." What a way to make both teams unhappy!

The Israelites of Elijah's day were like that weak umpire. For a while they served the Lord, then they followed Ahab—their most evil king to date (1 Kings 16:33)—in Baal worship. God directed His prophet Elijah (v. 36) to confront the 450 prophets of Baal in a showdown on Mount Carmel. He challenged the people to decide once and for all whom they would serve (v. 21).

The false prophets were on the spot. They could not call fire from a false god; the best they could hope for was that the people would remain indecisive. This is still Satan's best hope today. If he can convince people not to decide anything, he has convinced them to decide for him. After the prophets of Baal spent the day making fools of themselves, Elijah repaired an altar, killed a bull, and had the whole sacrifice doused three times with water to enhance the miracle God was going to perform. He then prayed a short prayer; God heard and answered. Imagine the fear in the hearts of the false prophets when they discovered that the Law declared they were to be executed (Deut. 13:1–11).

We are involved in a life-and-death struggle against sin and evil today. The stakes—our freedom, our nation, our families—are high. But if we will trust and reverence God, He will honor our faith. It's not too late to decide to serve the one true God.

Consider: *In what area are you unsure whether to trust God?*

Against All Odds

Read 2 Kings 6:8–23

"Don't be afraid. . . . Those who are with us are more than those who are with them." 2 Kings 6:16

One day in 1956, a right-hander named Carl Erskine was scheduled to pitch for the Dodgers against the New York Giants. Though his arm was very sore, Carl could not tell the manager he couldn't pitch. Totally discouraged, he simply prayed, *I have very little to offer; I may not even be able to warm up. Help me do the best with what I've got.*Then he began to throw. He got through the warm-up, the first inning, the fifth inning, and by the ninth inning, New York hadn't gotten a hit off him! When Alvin Dark grounded out and ended the game, Erskine finished the best performance of his career—a no-hitter. God had answered his simple prayer and changed his entire perspective.

The prophet Elisha also had a servant who needed a new perspective. When a foreign power (Aram) harassed Israel, God gave Elisha inside information concerning their troop movements. Elisha became one great Israelite superspy! Once Aram discovered Elisha's secret, they sent a large detachment of forces to capture him. When the servant saw this army he sank into despair. Looking through physical eyes, he fretted, "Oh, my lord, what shall we do?" Wise Elisha prayed that his servant might see the situation through spiritual eyes (v. 17). As the Lord opened his eyes, the servant saw the hills full of horses and chariots from heaven. Elisha and his servant were far stronger than they appeared.

Many times we feel inadequate for the task ahead. We look at the obstacles, see an impossible situation, and despair sets in. At such times, we need to remember to look at things from God's perspective. He has made all the armies of heaven available for our defense. All we need to do is to trust Him.

Consider: *Do you see problems through spiritual eyes or only through physical eyes?*

A Consistent Offense

"... the God of Israel says: I have heard your prayer. . . ."   2 Kings 19:20

A famous football coach was quoted as saying, "Only a grossly inferior team will ever depart from its strength to win." Consistent winners are those who execute basic plays well. Though a variety of formations may be used, a team always has those bread-and-butter plays to rely on in the clutch. Razzle-dazzle plays are occasionally effective but never the basis of a consistent offense.

Fortunately for Judah, Hezekiah went to his basic offense in an emergency. We are told that there was no king like Hezekiah among all the kings of Judah. This godly man trusted the Lord, did what was right, removed the relics of idolatry, and was obedient to the Lord. Because of this, the Lord was with him, and he was successful in everything he undertook (2 Kings 18:3–7). Nevertheless, one day the Assyrian commander under Sennacherib laid siege to Jerusalem and threatened both the people and their Lord. Rather than engage in verbal battle, Hezekiah took his problem before his Lord in prayer (v.14). He did not pray a long or complex prayer but simply praised God for who He was, pointed out the problem, and asked for help. God's answer through the prophet Isaiah was swift and sure. In one night the angel of the Lord personally killed 185 thousand Assyrians (v. 35). Sennacherib broke camp and withdrew.

Are you beset by an army of problems that threaten to overwhelm you? Our Lord is a mighty God and gracious to come to our rescue when we call on Him. It doesn't require a long, flowery prayer to gain the hearing of our loving heavenly Father. Simply lay out your problems to the Lord and release them to Him. His answer will arrive just in the nick of time.

Consider: *Under what conditions do you pray most simply and honestly to God?*

Don't Let Up Too Soon

Asa   Read 2 Chronicles 16

"For the eyes of the Lord range throughout the earth to strengthen those whose hearts are fully committed to him."   2 Chron. 16:9

Ex-Yankee manager Casey Stengel is remembered for such famous one-liners as "The ball game is not over until it's over." Though the statement seems ridiculous, there is profound truth in the thought that any team can come back until the last out is made or the final horn sounds. A team in the lead cannot become complacent; a team behind must not give up. The finish is crucial.

King Asa should have met Casey Stengel and listened to his advice. The king started his life and ruled his kingdom with much grace and wisdom. Second Chronicles 14 and 15 tells us that Asa was an upright king who was fully committed to God and led many righteous reforms. For thirty-six of Asa's forty-one years as king, Israel prospered because Asa led with a pure heart.

But neither Asa's life nor his reign was over yet. Late in his reign, Asa stopped relying on or even consulting God in his decisions. He trusted the pagan King Ben-Hadad instead of the Lord (v. 7). In severe illness at the end of life, Asa sought his doctor's help, but not his Lord's help. This great man of God could have saved himself much suffering and his country many lives if he had remembered the strength of Jehovah and had gone to Him in prayer. Though he ran the race well, he took God for granted and weakly finished his course. Asa forgot about the power of God that came through humble prayer. He lost God's strength when he forgot about His presence.

God is still looking for humble, committed hearts (v. 9). You may have run your race well so far, but finish as strongly as you began. Then you can say with Paul, "I have fought the good fight, I have finished the race, I have kept the faith" (2 Tim. 4:7).

Consider: *What project have you begun in total commitment that must be likewise completed?*

59

The Pressures of Success

Jehoshaphat   Read 2 Chronicles 20

"Do not be afraid or discouraged because of this vast army. For the battle is not yours, but God's."   2 Chron. 20:15

Sometimes the pressures of life become so intense that strong men and women despair and retreat. Financial pressures, job pressures, or home pressures can break down our endurance. Even the pressures of success can be overwhelming, as in the case of French tennis player Yannick Noah. Late in 1983, Noah called a news conference to explain his leaving Paris to live in New York City. Yannick, the world's fourth-ranked tennis player, wept as he said he could not handle the pressure of being an idol in France.

When King Jehoshaphat of Judah faced great external pressure from an advancing army, he proclaimed a time of fasting and praying (v. 3). Before the people, he poured out his heart to God (v. 12): "For we have no power to face this vast army that is attacking us. We do not know what to do, but our eyes are upon you." The secret of victory is found in this humble attitude.

What did God do? He calmly assured Jehoshaphat that it was God's business to protect His people and that the king was not to fear. It was not Jehoshaphat's personal fight; he was a steward in the affairs of God. All he had to do was stand firm and see God work (v. 17). As the people praised the Lord and obeyed, Jehovah decisively crushed their enemies.

Are you facing pressures today? Is it pressure that results from standing for God's principles, sharing Christ with others, or taking care of others? If so, the battle is not yours, but God's. If your pressure is from selfish desires to get more things or to advance higher on the social scale, quickly give these things to God, and this sort of pressure will cease. With your eyes on Him, relax in His powerful arms and you will see His deliverance.

Consider: *Are you trusting God or fighting your own battles?*

Pride and a Fall

But after Uzziah became powerful, his pride led to his downfall.

2 Chron. 26:16

Tom Landry of the Dallas Cowboys was quoted in *Sporting News* as saying: "I'm sure that we're all very different. But we each have our way of handling winning and losing. People are always talking about defeat. You have to handle winning, too. If you get overbloated, too proud of what you've accomplished, it's a good way to take a quick fall."

King Uzziah could have benefited from heeding Landry's words. After becoming king of Judah at age sixteen, he enjoyed a glorious fifty-two-year reign. He honored the Lord even more than his father had (v. 4). Uzziah sought God and His will through the godly Zechariah (v. 5). He must have been a good father because his son Jotham also did what was right in God's eyes and enjoyed a long and prosperous reign (2 Chron. 27). As a result of his faithfulness, God blessed both Israel and King Uzziah, and he became very powerful and famous.

But one day Uzziah let his pride get the best of him. He usurped the place of the priests and entered the temple to offer incense. Maybe he felt he could do a better job than the priests. Though he may have been right, it was not his calling. God had strictly forbidden anyone but descendants of Aaron to perform this function (1 Chron. 23:13). When reproved, Uzziah flew into a rage. God immediately chastised him with incurable leprosy, and the priests themselves hurried him out of the temple. Good King Uzziah remained isolated until his death.

Are your succeeding today? Praise God for all His blessings. But beware of pride because it will cause a rapid and painful fall.

Consider: *How can you guard against the pride of success?*

Judgment Delayed

Josiah   Read 2 Chronicles 34

"Because your heart was responsive and you humbled yourself before God
... your eyes will not see all the disaster I am going to bring on this place
and on those who live here."   2 Chron. 34:27–28

Any delayed-action play, such as a screen pass, is effective in
negating a hard-charging defensive football team. The onrushing
linemen penetrate as the quarterback fades deeper than usual,
waiting for a back to sift behind the defenders and into the clear.
Then the quarterback lofts a pass over the heads of the rushing
defenders, and the receiver follows his blockers downfield. Though
the attack is certain, it is postponed momentarily.

Decadence in Israel had reached new lows, so when King
Josiah discovered what God required of His people he knew
judgment was inevitable. Second Kings 23:25 records that no king
ever turned as completely to the Lord as did Josiah. Seeking God in
his youth (v. 3), he reformed the nation step-by-step. He destroyed
Israel's pagan shrines and six years later gave orders to repair
God's temple. During this time Hilkiah the priest discovered the
laws that God gave to Moses. When Josiah learned how deeply the
people had wronged God, he tore his robes in shame, which
showed his humility and grief and demonstrated a true love for God
and a desire to please Him. Did God still punish sin? Yes, but
because of Josiah's repentance, God delayed His judgment and
kept the nation free during Josiah's lifetime.

Americans who love God must grieve for our nation. The
consequences of sin—venereal disease, high suicide rates, family
breakdowns, and lawlessness—are everywhere. Sexual immoral-
ity, mass murders through abortion, tolerance of homosexuality
carry a high price tag. The Lord has every reason to destroy us, but
the story of Josiah gives reason for hope. If this generation will
repent, God may prolong our freedom.

Consider: *How much do you pray for our nation?*

The Best Kind of Coach

For Ezra had devoted himself to the study and observance of the Law of the Lord, and to teaching its decrees and laws in Israel.   Ezra 7:10

An outstanding coach not only knows the game he is teaching but continues to increase his knowledge. His credibility is also increased if he is able to demonstrate personally the skills of the sport. When these characteristics are present—knowledge, continued study, and demonstration—along with the ability to communicate with enthusiasm to his players, the coach has an excellent chance of successfully leading his team.

Ezra the priest would have been a very successful coach. During Israel's Babylonian captivity, many of God's prophets had passed from the scene. To revive the knowledge of God, Ezra went to the Scriptures and studied diligently about God and what He expected of His people. Not only did Ezra know God and His Word, but he also kept God's laws and communicated them to others. Because of his diligence to do and teach the will of God, the hand of the Lord was on him (v. 28).

What kind of coach in God's kingdom are you? You need not be a staff member of some church or Christian ministry to coach God's people. The Lord's plan is for all believers to serve Him full-time with whatever skill and position He has given them. Through consistent study, do you first know God's Word and then apply it in daily life? Do you desire to communicate His truth to others? The more of God's Word you share with others, the better you will understand it and the more truths God will reveal to you.

Plan now to speak to someone about what God has spoken through His Word. Make sure you are applying His truth personally, and God will greatly use you.

Consider: *What truths from God's Word will you share with someone this week?*

63

Enthusiasm Wins

Nehemiah   Read Nehemiah 8:1–12

". . . for the joy of the Lord is your strength."   Neh. 8:10

Many ingredients are needed to produce an outstanding football team. There is the technical knowledge of the coach, team organization, and the physical talent of each player. Though all these are important, no team ever achieved its potential without a unifying team spirit. Players who care for their teammates, who place others before themselves, and who excel under adversity are a tremendous asset. A spirit of enthusiasm and joy carries them further when fatigue threatens.

As a wise governor of Israel, Nehemiah recognized the need for a joyful spirit in the nation he ruled. Gathering the people together to hear the Word of God read by Ezra (v. 3) and explained by the Levites (v. 8), Nehemiah imparted the technical knowledge of the Law to his people. He had seen that the people were settled in their towns and he assembled them in organized fashion (v. 1). But the mechanics were only part of their worship. The tender-hearted people began to weep when they saw how far short of God's standard they had fallen. Their spirit of humility led Nehemiah to encourage them to eat, drink, give to others, and to celebrate their newly found understanding of God (v. 12). Their strength to carry on depended not upon Nehemiah's knowledge or organization, as vital as these were, but upon their rejoicing in the Lord (v. 10) and in realizing His greatness.

In our Christian lives, God's Holy Spirit produces the joy and enthusiasm needed to overcome obstacles. That joy gives us strength to carry on in adversity. The more we understand about God, the more joy we will possess. That's why having His Word carefully explained to us regularly is so vital. Then we can come into His presence with thanksgiving and praise. Knowing God brings a joy that the world does not give and cannot take away.

Consider: *In what ways does the joy of the Lord strengthen you?*

The Right Time and Place

"And who knows but that you have come to royal position for such a time as this?"
Esth. 4:14

The miracle play of the 1983 NFL season occurred on November 20, 1983. The game was between Atlanta and San Francisco, and the Forty-niners had it won until the last play of the game. With hope all but gone, Steve Bartkowski of the Falcons launched a 47-yard desperation pass to the Forty-niners' goal line where it was tipped twice, bounced backward, and landed in the waiting arms of Billy "White Shoes" Johnson. White Shoes eluded two tacklers and planted the ball on the goal line for a 28–24 Falcon victory! Johnson was in the right place at the right time, saved the game, and became a hero.

Queen Esther also found herself in the right place at the right time. As a Jewish girl who was elevated to queen during the rule of the Medes and Persians, Esther was in a position of influence. Tragedy struck when Satan, through Haman, plotted the annihilation of the Jewish people. Would Esther risk her position for the glory of God and to save her people?

At this point, Mordecai, Esther's foster father and a Jew of great faith, reminded her that this was possibly the very reason God had made her queen. After prayer and fasting, Esther approached the king at the risk of her life and interceded for the Jewish nation. God changed his heart, the nation was spared, and great celebration followed.

You may not be king or queen of an empire. You may never be in position to catch a tipped pass for a game-winning touchdown. But if you know Christ, God has put you in a certain place to serve Him and others. When opportunities to stand for righteousness come, don't let them slip away. He will use you and greatly reward your efforts.

Consider: *Where has God placed you to speak out for Him?*

65

Hang in There

Job   Read Job 42:1-6

"I know that you can do all things; no plan of yours can be thwarted."
Job 42:2

In *They Call Me Coach,* John Wooden has much to say about the importance of patience and perseverance: "In game play, it has always been my philosophy that patience will win out. By that, I mean patience to follow our game plan. If we do believe in it, we will wear the opposition down and will get them. If we break away from our style, however, and play their style, we're in trouble. And if we let our emotions command the game rather than our reason, we will not function effectively."

Long ago, a righteous man named Job learned a valuable lesson of patience when he was allowed to suffer. His story is one of the most debated and misunderstood stories of history. A blameless man who feared God, Job had been blessed with a large family and material riches (Job 1:1-3). Though he had wealth, power, and fame, he remained true to God. Yet, God allowed Job to lose everything, including his physical health. His wife and friends were of no help, and he suffered alone. Job did not understand: He questioned God's justice and protested his circumstances. Finally, after hearing of the sovereign majesty of God from Elihu (Job 32-37) and from the Lord Himself (Job 38-41), Job realized that he could trust God no matter what the circumstances. Though a righteous man, Job still had room to grow, to learn patience during hard times, to experience what he had previously only heard (v. 5).

Are you frustrated by repeated losses, hurts, and circumstances you cannot understand? Though you may never know until you get to heaven how or why things happen, by God's grace you can accept trials and praise God. It's God's way of developing His character in you.

Consider: *Through which trials has God increased your patience?*

66

A Reason to Hope

"In the year that King Uzziah died, I saw the Lord. . . ."   Isa. 6:1

Late every summer, major-league baseball teams increase the size of their rosters to enable players to get a feel for what it's like to play for the big team. Only a few days in the big time gives a man hope and encouragement to persist in his efforts to make next year's club. The theory is that everyone needs a vision of what it's like to succeed.

God knew that His future star Isaiah would need encouragement if he were to fulfill his calling. So God gave Isaiah a vision of His glory. While he did not actually see the essence of God (John 1:18), Isaiah did see a manifestation of the Mighty One. Seraphs with six wings ministered to the exalted Lord. They covered their faces (humility), their feet (reverence), and flew (service) as they praised Him. Singing of His holiness ("Holy, Holy, Holy") and His power ("Lord Almighty"), their voices shook the temple. What majesty to behold!

When Isaiah saw God, he saw himself as he was—a man of unclean speech unable to speak of such glory. In fact, when a man truly sees God, he is convicted of all lying, gossip, slander, and shady stories. Having confessed his sin, Isaiah received cleansing, heard God speak to him, and responded in the strength of the Lord. He became the greatest of the Old Testament prophets—a master statesman and spokesman for God.

We have a problem today. Few people have time to wait on God, to listen to Him speak, and to catch a vision of His greatness. As a result, few Christians have any power for living. Before the concerns of life sweep you away, invest time in what really counts—knowing the almighty King. As you meditate on the Lord, all worry, tension, and stagnation is replaced by His glory.

Consider: *Have you caught a glimpse of God's greatness?*

Top Draft Choice

"Before I formed you in the womb I knew you, before you were born I set you apart. . . ."   Jer. 1:5

The Denver Broncos' top draft choice of 1983 has become one of the league's best quarterbacks. John Elway, the rifle-armed Stanford grad, was not only highly sought by Denver, but he was also reportedly insured before ever playing in the NFL. A spokesman for Sports Insurance International of Houston, the largest insuror of athletes and entertainers in North America, indicated that "at least six figures" would be required to write a policy on Elway.

According to Scripture, our sovereign Lord drafts and insures men even before birth for the accomplishment of His purpose. Jeremiah ("appointed by God") was an example. God's plan, laid out in God's own mind, preceded His call to the prophet. Jeremiah was to prophesy to national leaders, warning them of the consequences of their continued sin. This plan and call of God (not education, wealth, or position) enabled Jeremiah to endure and to succeed in his mission. As the Lord put knowledge in his mind and words in his mouth, He also provided the grace and power for His prophet to fulfill his destiny.

If you are a Christian, plan to use your life for His glory. His investment in you is high. First He created you; then He paid for you; and then He purchased you with the precious blood of His Son. He also gave His Holy Spirit as your down payment on a new home in heaven (2 Cor. 5:5). He expects you to be controlled by the Spirit (Eph. 5:18). He promises to finish the work that He has begun in all His children (Phil. 1:6). What a privilege to be chosen by the Master Coach for His team—the greatest in the universe!

Consider: *What has God chosen you to do for His glory?*

Shafted in a Well

Jeremiah   Read Jeremiah 37:1—38:6

So they took Jeremiah and put him into the cistern. . . .   Jer. 38:6

No matter how successful an athlete's career has been, they all have days they would just as soon forget. The Giants' Christy Matthewson once pitched sixty-eight consecutive walkless innings. On June 7, 1906, however, he walked six Cub batters in one inning and was beaten 19–0! On April 28, 1934, Hall of Fame outfielder Goose Goslin, who had a .316 lifetime batting average, hit into four consecutive double plays against Cleveland. In 1975, the same thing happened to Joe Torre, an outstanding catcher-infielder who four years earlier had one of the best years ever enjoyed by a pro—230 hits, 137 RBI's and a .363 average. The great Stan Musial once fell while chasing a fly ball, and as it hit him in the head, two runs scored! Even those at the top occasionally hit rock bottom.

The prophet Jeremiah was faithful to God. As with all true prophets, every prediction he made came to pass. It was his assignment to warn Judah of Babylon's impending capture of Jerusalem because of the idolatry of the people. Over and over, he cried out to his people, but they paid no attention (v. 2). After the siege began, he was falsely accused, arrested, beaten, imprisoned, and later thrown neck deep into a muddy cistern, according to Josephus. What a reward for being faithful to Jehovah! It was certainly a day Jeremiah would have liked to forget.

The Israelites consistently tortured, killed, or ignored the prophets God sent them (Matt. 23:34–37). Note Jeremiah's reaction to this treatment. "I called on your name, O Lord, from the depth of the pit. You came near when I called you and you said, 'Do not fear'" (Lam. 3:55, 57). On a day when nothing seemed to go his way, Jeremiah remained faithful to God. And God remained faithful to him; He freed him from the miry clay.

Consider: *How do you adjust to a bad day?*

Measuring Success

        Read Ezekiel 2

"And whether they listen or fail to listen . . . they will know that a prophet has been among them."   Ezek. 2:5

Veteran coach Dal Shealy knows what life is like on both sides of the spectrum in college football. He has coached a nationally ranked team and been named Coach of the Year. On the other hand, his 1982 Richmond Spiders experienced a nightmarish 0–10 season. Though times were hard, his faith remained. He spoke of his priorities in *Sharing the Victory*.

> . . . God's plan of success is different than the world's. Most coaches would consider an 0–10 season a disaster, yet God was still in control. We've had some storms but our foundation hasn't washed away because it's built on the Rock. I like Philippians 1:6: "Being confident of this, that He who began a good work in you will carry it on to completion until the day of Christ Jesus."

The prophet Ezekiel ("God strengthens") also had a tough assignment. In 593 B.C., during the Babylonian captivity, God sent him to tell the rebellious Israelites that the reason for their captivity was their idolatry. God warned Ezekiel that he would be persecuted for his pronouncement, but Ezekiel's commission was to be faithful, regardless of whether or not the people turned back to God (v. 5).

There is nothing wrong with desiring success. But God measures success differently than the world does, and He doesn't use a scoreboard. He is pleased if we faithfully do what He instructs, when He tells us to do it, and how He wants it done. This is success for the believer.

Are you hung up over wins and losses, money and material, power and prestige? Then serve God because of who He is, not because of what He has! Be faithful regardless, because faithfulness is the true measure of success.

Consider: *According to God's criteria, how are you succeeding?*

Two-Minute Warning

". . . I have made you a watchman for the house of Israel. . . ."   Ezek. 3:16

The excitement of a football game is enhanced by a warning issued to both benches when two minutes remain in the contest. Strategies are planned around this period of time, and each team gives a last all-out effort to win. A true champion rises to his highest level when the game is on the line.

Ezekiel, one of God's champions, rose to the top when called by God during Israel's Babylonian captivity. God held Ezekiel responsible to warn the Jewish people of sin's consequences, to warn the wicked to turn from sin to God, and to warn the righteous man to continue in righteousness. Ezekiel's preparation was to know the Word of God. He was commanded to "eat" the scroll (v.1). His commission was to be a watchman—a dangerous position during wartime—and to take orders from God and give warning to the people.

We may have less than two minutes left on God's time clock. Every believer in the Lord Jesus Christ is called to be a watchman for the lives of others. We are not to live for ourselves; we must warn the unsaved of the danger of not believing. After removing the "beam in our own eye," we are to warn other Christians who have fallen into sinful habits. This must be done humbly (Gal. 6:1) and preferably in private (Matt. 18:15). Genuine love will prompt us to alert our friends to dangerous patterns in their lives.

At the conclusion of a ball game, the action usually becomes more intense as both sides struggle for victory. How intense is your concern for others and the things of God as the game of life winds down? Do you love others enough to warn them of the consequences of their sin?

Consider: *To whom would God have you give warning in love today?*

Cool in the Furnace

Shadrach, Meshach, and Abednego   Read Daniel 3

" . . . we will not serve your gods or worship the image of gold you have set up."   Dan. 3:18

The wishbone triple option is a great offense when executed to perfection. The strategy of a team that runs the wishbone is to stay even or ahead on the scoreboard and control the football. Just about the worst thing that can happen to an option team is to fall behind in the second half, to let the opponent set the tempo of the game, and to leave their game plan. Once the team leaves the game plan and resorts to passing, the option team's chances of victory are drastically reduced. It is imperative that the game plan be completed.

As captives in a foreign land, three young Hebrew men were faced with extreme circumstances and tempted to leave their game plan. According to Daniel 1, Shadrach, Meshach, and Abednego were strong, handsome, intelligent, and loyal to the God of Israel. The three purposed in their hearts to remain faithful to Him, no matter what the cost. That resolve was soon tested, as King Nebuchadnezzar threatened to burn alive anyone who refused to worship his statue. Knowing that God was able to rescue them, yet unsure whether it was in His will to do so, the trio stuck to their game plan of faithfulness to Him (vv. 16–18).

Furiously, Nebuchadnezzar had the furnace heated seven times hotter and the three youths thrown in. But instead of death, they were preserved in the presence of a fourth person who many scholars believe was Jesus Christ Himself!

Are you amid trying times and tempted to leave the game plan of loyalty and service to Christ? Hang in there! Don't quit! God will never let you down. In the fiery furnace of affliction, you will experience the presence of the living God and your faith will be substantiated.

Consider: *Why is it best to stick to God's game plan?*

72

Challenge of a Lifetime

Daniel   Read Daniel 6

"My God sent his angel, and he shut the mouths of the lions."   Dan. 6:22

Freshman Bernie Kosar, a young Jewish lad from Ohio, faced the sports challenge of his life in the 1984 Orange Bowl when he led his Miami Hurricanes into battle against powerful Nebraska. The top-ranked Cornhuskers blitzed defensive backs, shifted defenses before the snap, and even switched jerseys in an attempt to confuse the young quarterback. Nevertheless, Kosar led his team to an exciting 31–30 upset victory and the national championship! Nebraska cornerback Dave Burke commented about Kosar to the *Miami Herald:* "Even with our number switches, he played smart. He didn't play like a freshman. He played like a senior."

A long time ago, another Jewish boy faced a great challenge. His name was Daniel, and he was known for his exceptional qualities of leadership, honesty, trustworthiness, and loyalty to God. Because of the jealousy of peers, Daniel was confronted with the ultimate test—whether to keep his faith or save his own skin. The Bible says that Daniel continued to pray with thanksgiving to the Lord (v. 10). Though the trap was sprung and Daniel was thrown to the lions by the gullible King Darius, God acted on behalf of His faithful servant. His angel protected Daniel all night while the king tossed and turned in the palace. When the king found Daniel alive at daybreak, he rescued him and had his accusers tossed to the lions instead. Before they reached bottom, they were torn limb from limb! Because of his trust in God during adversity (v. 23), Daniel was saved and prospered during Darius's reign.

Are you facing hungry lions that threaten to eat you? Are financial pressures, job conflicts, school work, or family problems on the prowl? Remember Daniel's poise under pressure as he went to his source of strength. God spared Daniel; He can spare you, too.

Consider: *How are you handling pressure?*

Unlikely Hero

Amos   Read Amos 7

"... I was neither a prophet nor a prophet's son. ..."   Amos 7:14

The World Series often provides the setting for obscure ballplayers to emerge as heroes. Al Weis, a good defensive second baseman with a .219 season batting average, stole the show as he led the '69 Mets over Baltimore. Gene Tenace, an unsung catcher, collected eight hits (four homers) and drove in nine runs for Oakland as the A's defeated the Reds in 1972. More recently, Rick Dempsey hit .385 in leading the Orioles over Philadelphia in 1983.

Amos, another unlikely hero, was sent by God in His final effort to turn Israel from her mad dash toward destruction. Two hundred years earlier, the northern kingdom (Israel) had set up a government with calf worship as its religion. Pagan practices were rampant (1 Kings 12:25–33). In 751 B.C., while Amos gave his warning of impending doom, he prayed for the people. Twice God mercifully took another course (vv. 1–6), but their sin finally exhausted His patience. The apostate religious ruler Amaziah tried to discredit Amos (a layman) by misrepresenting him to the king (vv. 10–13). Then he tried to get Amos to take his preaching elsewhere, insinuating that such a blunt person as Amos shouldn't frequent the king's court.

Amos stood his ground. Though he had no thought of being a prophet nor had he any religious training, God had taken Amos from his farming duties (vv. 14–15) and was using him in place of the corrupt religious leaders. His calling and authority came directly from God. The Lord pronounced a curse on Amaziah and his family for opposing the shepherd-prophet Amos.

Ever feel that you're an unlikely person to be used by God? Remember, you have access to as much of God's Word as any pastor. God can and will use you whether or not you are a man of the cloth.

Consider: *In what unlikely ways is God using you?*

74

The Uncertainty of It All

When Joseph woke up, he did what the angel of the Lord had commanded him. . . .   Matt. 1:24

When Dallas punter Danny White was injured during the 1984 football season, the Cowboys sought a replacement. Personnel director Gil Brandt thought of ex-Tennessee kicker John Warren. They found John delivering produce. He rushed to Knoxville, boarded a plane for Dallas, and punted in Sunday's game. Before the season was over, he had been released, picked up again as White's injuries reoccurred, and released again.

Joseph was directed by God amid many similar up-and-down situations. Not much is recorded of Jesus' earthly guardian, but we know he was an honorable man who followed God's leading. A relatively poor carpenter, Joseph was engaged to Mary when he learned of her pregnancy. Jewish engagements were permanent marriage contracts, though the couple lived apart during a one-year waiting period. Joseph decided to break off the engagement quietly, but God sent an angel in the first of four dreams (v. 20) to guide him. The angel reassured Joseph that the child was the Son of God, not fathered by any human, and that he should not fear to marry Mary. After Jesus' birth, Joseph was warned in a second dream (Matt. 2:13) to flee to Egypt because King Herod was murdering all male babies under two years of age in a jealous effort to kill the Messiah. Again Joseph obeyed. In a third dream (Matt. 2:19) he was told to return to Israel in fulfillment of ancient messianic prophecy (Mic. 5:2). In a fourth dream, the angel directed him to Nazareth in fulfillment of still another prophecy. In all these circumstances, Joseph obeyed quickly and consistently.

Do changes cause turmoil in your life? Are you able to maintain a calm obedience to God through life's ups and downs? Change is one of the few things we can be sure of on this earth.

Consider: *Of what things are you certain in this uncertain world?*

Beware of Easy Living

John the Baptist   Read Matthew 3:1–12

In those days John the Baptist came, preaching in the Desert of Judea and saying, "Repent, for the kingdom of heaven is near."   Matt. 3:1–2

The softening effect of easy living creeps upon all who are not alert. Eddie Arcaro, one of America's most successful jockeys, learned this when he retired in 1962. A reporter asked him if he still got up early to walk his horses around the track before the dew was off. Arcaro frankly admitted, "It becomes difficult to get up early once a guy starts wearing silk pajamas."

Many religious leaders had fallen into a soft life when John the Baptist came on the scene. What a contrast John was! He dressed in camel's hair and he ate locusts and wild honey. This tough preacher was a throwback to the ancient prophets and a forerunner of the Messiah. He probably spent about thirty years in relative seclusion, approximately one and a half years preaching, and another year in prison. The significance of John's life was his message. Though silent for four hundred years, God did not quietly sneak the Messiah on Israel. He used John ("Jehovah is gracious") to broadcast the coming of Christ and His kingdom. The requirement to enter the kingdom was repentance: change your heart and mind; decide to do things God's way. Many repented, but as a nation, Israel refused. The religious rulers grew hostile and accused John of demon possession (Matt. 11:18). Because of his bold reproof of Herod's sin (Matt. 14:4), he was later beheaded.

God still requires repentance. We must change our minds concerning His Son and let Christ change our hearts. Not to acknowledge sin assures us of God's judgment. God used John because he would not compromise the message. And He will use us if we will stay true to His Word and not grow soft on sin.

Consider: *What "soft" areas of your life need to be strengthened?*

Socially Unacceptable

"For I have not come to call the righteous, but sinners."   Matt. 9:13

Over the years, the Los Angeles Raiders have become known as the bad guys of the NFL. Often, they have taken the outlaws from other teams and gotten them to play together well enough to be competitive. Their rough, intimidating style and their black jerseys with skull and crossbones on the helmets have enhanced the image. One player on another team, when accused of being a renegade, denied it by saying that if he were a problem he'd "have been traded to Oakland long ago!"

Several of Jesus' disciples were social outcasts. To the dismay of religious leaders, Jesus spent time with those who didn't fit their mold. His calling of Matthew, the tax collecter, was quite a shock; no group was more hated than tax collectors. They often demanded more than their due and were regarded as traitors for selling themselves to the Roman government for personal gain. To the Jews, they were as low as Gentiles, harlots, and sinners. But Jesus, ignoring the scorn of religious leaders, called Matthew, and Matthew left his lucrative business to follow the Master (Luke 5:28). Formerly known as Levi, Matthew ("gift of God") received a new life and a new name. He invited Jesus to his home for a great feast and to meet his friends—other tax men and sinners. He was not ashamed of Jesus, and Jesus was not ashamed to be seen with him or any other sinner.

We owe much to this IRS agent who gave up his profession for Christ. He was the first to write an account of the Lord's teachings for the early church and the only one to record the Sermon on the Mount. But most of all, he encourages us to share Christ with the outcasts of society, for whom the Lord came to give abundant and eternal life.

Consider: *When you are criticized for the company you keep how do you respond?*

Unlikely Teammate

These are the names of the twelve apostles . . . Simon the Zealot. . . .
Matt. 10:2–4

Conflicts between people who are different are not rare in the sports world. In 1892, world heavyweight champion John L. Sullivan refused to fight an outstanding black challenger. "I will not fight a Negro. I never have and I never will," he said. In 1910, the skillful and outspoken Jack Johnson, a black boxer, flaunted his superiority by demolishing a bevy of "white hopes" at a time of blatant racism. After he defeated a white boxer in a highly publicized fight, race riots broke out in several large cities.

It has never been common for people of opposite viewpoints to get along. That's why Jesus' choice of Simon the Zealot was so extraordinary. The Zealots were a fanatical sect of Jewish patriots who fanned resentment against Rome with bloody outbursts. Their hatred for Rome led to the destruction of the Jewish nation in 70 A.D., when the Romans grew weary of Jewish hostility. Zealots led the holdout at Masada, where 960 Jews perished by their own hand rather than surrender to Rome. Simon left this group of revolutionaries to join the greatest of all revolutionaries. But in joining Christ's side, Simon had to forsake his own passionate beliefs. Imagine Simon working and living with Matthew, who accepted Roman rule and even collected taxes for them. What a change of heart these men must have had. Jesus' law of love destroyed the strife that would have led Simon to plant a knife in Matthew's back!

Not much is said of Simon in Scripture. But his example proves that no disagreement is so big that it cannot be healed by Christ's love. Black and white, Jew and Gentile, rich and poor are one in Christ and can serve peacefully together when they are in love with the Lord.

Consider: *How can you love those who are different?*

Handling Doubt

When John heard in prison what Christ was doing, he sent his disciples to ask him, "Are you the one who was to come, or should we expect someone else?"   Matt. 11:2–3

Discouragement is common to every member of the human race. Basketball great Rick Barry was once cut from his junior-high basketball team! Major-league pitcher Craig Lefferts was cut from the University of Arizona. Tom Landry's first Dallas Cowboy team finished 1–13! Though doubts must have entered each man's mind, they shook off negative thoughts.

Even John the Baptist became discouraged and frustrated. This bold yet humble preacher had widely proclaimed the Lord Jesus as the Messiah sent by God to establish His kingdom. John insisted that his own mission was only to announce the coming of the Messiah (John 1:23). He was so sure of his message that he was willing to lose himself in Jesus, taking a back seat to the one who was greater (John 3:30). But John had a problem. He was in jail for denouncing the sin of a governor (Matt. 14:3). Sitting in a dingy prison cell, he needed reassurance. He had believed that Jesus would usher in a new kingdom and punish sin. Yet, here he was under lock and key, while Jesus continued to teach! As questions flooded his mind, he asked Jesus for answers, and Jesus reassured Him by pointing out the miracles he had performed (vv. 4–6).

Like John, most of us doubt God at one time or another. Doubt is a matter of the mind, a difficulty in understanding; unbelief is a matter of the will, an act of disobedience. John did not let his doubt become unbelief; instead he took it to Jesus, who pointed out the evidence that He was indeed the Messiah.

How do you handle doubt? The best way is to go to God's Word and pray. As He reminds you of the Son and His work on your behalf, your faith will be strengthened.

Consider: *What are some doubts you need to resolve?*

A Crucial Call

"You are the Christ, the Son of the living God."   Matt. 16:16

What a thrill for a coach to make a right call in the clutch! It may be an end sweep away from a slanting defense in football, a curve ball away from a power hitter in baseball, or a man-to-man press against a slower team in basketball. When the call is right for a crucial situation, satisfaction and success surely follow.

Simon Peter once made a crucial call in the clutch. When public opinion of the Lord Jesus was declining and open hostility increasing, the Master Coach gave His disciples a pregame quiz concerning His identity. "Who do you say I am?" He asked. Peter, the pile of shifting sand who would later become a rock, uttered a great statement: "You are the Christ, the Son of the living God!" What a call! After Jesus commended him, the Lord (in a play on words) continued, "You are Peter [*petros:* a fragment of stone or rock] and on this rock [*petra:* the whole rock itself—the statement Peter had just made concerning Jesus as the Christ] I will build my church, and the gates of hell [physical death] will not overcome it." Jesus said He would give Peter the "keys of the kingdom of heaven." Peter would make the way of salvation clear to others by spreading the news that Jesus was the Messiah.

Peter's good call in the clutch originated with God, who laid the cornerstone for our salvation in Christ (1 Peter 2:4–8). No other foundation could be laid (1 Cor. 2:11). Though Peter was named "rock" (John 1:42) when he was not very rocklike, he was willing to move ahead with the Lord. That trait is very pleasing to God.

Consider: *Who do you say that Jesus is?*

Betrayed by a Friend

Judas Iscariot   Read Matthew 26:14–25

"But woe to that man who betrays the Son of Man! It would be better for him if he had not been born." Matt. 26:24

One of the ugliest incidents in sports history occurred in the 1919 World Series between the Reds and the White Sox. The affair is now known as the Black Sox Scandal because it involved the bribery of eight Sox players by professional gamblers to throw the series to Cincinnati. The players involved were forever banned from baseball. In testimony before the grand jury, pitcher Eddie Cicotte confessed, "I am through with baseball. I'm going to lose myself somewhere and never touch another ball. I feel sorry to have brought this disgrace to my wife and children . . . I'd give a million dollars to undo what I've done."

Likewise, Judas Iscariot "wore the same uniform" as his teammates in appearance but he was never part of their team. Judas was trusted—he was treasurer of the group—but he never trusted Christ. He was more in love with the idea of ruling than with the Ruler; more in love with money than with the Messiah.

Evildoers among the children of God are nothing new. People can attend church, pray, read their Bibles, even witness to others without being saved. Judas probably preached, healed, even cast out demons (Mark 3:14–19). But why did Jesus choose Judas to wear the uniform when he had no heart for the team? First, Judas, though responsible for his actions, fulfilled prophecy regarding the Messiah's death (Ps. 41:9). Second, his example shows that we can serve Christ without ever knowing Him. Finally, it shows that Jesus knows how we feel when betrayed by a trusted friend.

Do you know the Lord as your personal Savior or are you using pious actions to make you look like a team member? Remember, you can serve Him without loving Him, but you cannot love Him without serving Him.

Consider: *How much do your outward actions reflect your inward character?*

Bad Habits Are Hard to Break

Peter   Read Matthew 26:69–75

Then he began to call down curses on himself and he swore to them, "I don't know the man!"   Matt. 26:74

Very few athletes execute proper fundamentals all the time, so knowledgeable coaching can be a great help. But every once in a while old habit patterns surface in the heat of battle, and a skilled player reverts back to old ways of performing! The results are disheartening for both player and coach.

Though Peter had been personally coached by Jesus, he was not exempt from reverting to old behavior. In fact, before Pentecost, all the disciples fluctuated between spiritual boldness (as they anticipated the establishment of Christ's kingdom) and carnal fears (as they saw Jesus' popularity decline). The attack on Peter came not through a threatening Roman soldier, but through the offhand question of a teasing girl. She didn't question his spiritual allegiance, just his physical presence. Peter responded to her spur-of-the-moment question with a spur-of-the-moment lie, which he repeated three times. As the cock crowed and Jesus looked upon him from an overhanging balcony (Luke 22:61), Peter remembered his Lord's prediction and plunged into the depths of despair. This moment of deep discouragement became a turning point in Peter's life.

Have you done something that you deeply regret? It may have been a momentary experience, but the effects were far-reaching. You may have faced criticism and hurt as a result. You may have wept bitter tears of repentance as Peter wept (v. 75). If so, thank God for His forgiveness and go on. As one writer put it, "Peter found the forgiveness beyond reason that can meet the sin beyond excuse." The same Lord who restored Peter will establish and strengthen you.

Consider: *What past habits has God removed from your life?*

Willing to Risk It All

Read Matthew 27:57–61

As evening approached, there came a rich man from Arimathea, named Joseph, who had himself become a disciple of Jesus.   Matt. 27:57

As salaries for professional athletes escalate, more and more of them become rich. Yet, their means of wealth is temporary and risky because a career can end with the snap of a bone or the tear of a ligament. A lot of rich men are playing a lot of risky games under a lot of constant pressure. Some can handle it; others cannot.

A rich man named Joseph put himself in a pressured situation when he asked for the body of Jesus. Joseph was a prominent member of a council called the Sanhedrin (Mark 15:43), which had condemned the Lord. Though he had opposed the death sentence for Jesus (Luke 23:51), Joseph remained a secret disciple out of fear of the Jews (John 19:38). The death of Christ, however, had an amazing effect. While Jesus' visible disciples fled, Joseph and Nicodemus (John 19:38–39) boldly stepped forward to identify with the crucified King! It was risky business for two men who had nothing to gain and perhaps everything—including their lives—to lose. Joseph's request amounted to an open confession of loyalty to the Lord Jesus. His request easily could have been refused, since Joseph was no relative of Jesus. Furthermore, he risked ceremonial defilement through contact with a dead body. Clearly, his relationship to Jesus had become more important than his religion!

How do you handle the pressure when identification with Jesus is potentially costly and you have nothing to gain personally? Is your love for Him strong enough to motivate the loyal response He deserves from you? Don't let your affluence rob you of the joy of risking all for the Savior.

Consider: *What are you willing to risk for Jesus? What are you not willing to risk?*

An Interruption at Training Camp

Greek Woman   Read Mark 7:24–30

She begged Jesus to drive the demon out of her daughter.   Mark 7:26

One of basketball's greatest coaches, Adolph Rupp of the University of Kentucky, demanded such concentration on the part of his players that he would not allow them to talk during practice. "I have these boys about two hours a day and I don't want them talking about their girls or cars. I want them concentrating on basketball," he said. Rupp's own concentration was one of the things that made him a great coach.

Apparently, the only time our Lord Jesus left Palestine was when He traveled to Tyre (Lebanon) to instruct His disciples privately. Jesus wanted the complete concentration of the Twelve during their training camp, but He couldn't keep His presence secret. His reputation for miracles preceded Him, so when a certain Greek woman saw Him, she didn't hesitate to interrupt Him. She went boldly to the Master, fell at His feet, and begged for deliverance for her daughter, who was demon possessed. How did Jesus handle this interruption? Without criticizing her, He explained that His mission was first to His disciples and to Israel (v. 27). He referred to helping her as giving "children's bread to dogs" ("little house pets"), and it was not customary to interrupt practice (or a family meal) to feed house pets from the table. But the woman persisted. She asked for the "crumbs under the table" (v. 28). Our loving Savior couldn't resist such great faith and humility. He healed her daughter. Because of her humble importunity in interceding for her daughter, the woman's desire was granted.

We, too, can bring each concern to the Master Coach. With persistence and humility, let us bring every request boldly before His throne of grace (Heb. 4:16).

Consider: *How patient are you when someone interrupts your concentration?*

"Express Written Consent"

". . . we told him to stop because he was not one of us."   Mark 9:38

During every televised Monday-night football game, Dandy Don Meredith reads the following announcement with as much enthusiasm as he can muster: "This telecast is presented by the authority of the National Football League, which is solely responsible for its contents. Any publication, retransmission, or other use of the pictures, descriptions, or accounts of this game without the express written consent of the National Football League is prohibited." The statement describes the legitimate authority of the NFL over rights to their games. Without such control, chaos would result.

No one has such exclusive rights to the propagation of the gospel. But one day John came across a man he didn't know who was using Jesus' name to drive out demons. Because he was not of their group and the apostle was intolerant of others' works, John rebuked him. When the indignant apostle stormed off and reported the incident to Jesus, the Master Coach quickly set him straight by saying, "Whoever is not against us is for us." There was no room for religious exclusionism, and no one had a right to hoard the gospel.

What a word for believers and churches today. Though the policy may be unspoken, many churches in America exclude those of another skin color from fellowship. They forget that God's kingdom includes people of every tribe and nation (Rev. 5:9). By their elaborate clothing, others turn their church services into fashion shows, excluding those of lesser means by making them feel inferior. Still others become high-minded about their denomination, looking down on those who attend other churches. God hates denominationalism as much as He hates snobbery or racism.

Consider: *In what ways are you exclusive about your beliefs?*

Leading by Serving

James and John   Read Mark 10:35–45

". . . whoever wants to become great among you must be your servant, and whoever wants to be first must be slave of all." Mark 10:43–44

In tennis, the player who serves best has the greatest chance of winning, since every point is started with a serve. If a player wins every game he serves, the only way he can lose is in the tiebreaker. To have a good serve, the player must be consistent; if he doesn't get the first serve in play, he must rely on a weaker, slower second serve. A good server gets his first serve in play about seventy percent of the time.

Those who would become spiritually great must also be consistent servers. Jesus taught and demonstrated that the best form of leadership is serving others. Two brothers, James and John, had trouble understanding this teaching. Nevertheless, these men, nicknamed Sons of Thunder for their violent demeanor and selfish ambition (Luke 9:51–55), were transformed by Jesus for the glory of God. John ("grace of the Lord") was physically strong and of superior intellect, but he was especially intolerant. He was transformed, however, and later wrote five books of our New Testament, dwelling on the love of God. He became known as "the disciple Jesus loved." Little is written about James, but we do know he was the first martyred apostle, killed by Herod in 44 A.D. (Acts 12:1–3). Some historians write that the officer who guarded James was so impressed by James's courage and consistency that he repented of his own sin and apologized to James for his brutal treatment. The officer publicly confessed Christ and was beheaded with James.

Both men came a long way from the brash kids who sought the highest positions in the kingdom. They learned, as we must, that the best leadership is that which serves others most consistently. Once transformed, they became dynamic tools for good in the hands of the Master Coach.

Consider: *How can you improve your serve?*

Too Small to Gain Attention

Bartimaeus   Read Mark 10:46–52

"Go," said Jesus, "your faith has healed you." Immediately he received his sight and followed Jesus along the road.   Mark 10:52

One of the greatest quarterbacks in NFL history was an athletic outcast after high school. A skinny 138 pounds, Johnny Unitas was rejected by Notre Dame and Indiana. Fortunately, the University of Louisville gave him a chance, and the gamble paid off. After college, however, Johnny Unitas again found himself rejected, as he was cut by the Pittsburgh Steelers. While playing sandlot football in Pittsburgh for six dollars a game, Johnny was spotted by a Baltimore Colt scout who gave him a tryout. This time he made the team, became a starter, and in eighteen NFL seasons passed for 40,239 yards. In 1979–80, the castoff quarterback was inducted into the Hall of Fame.

Another outcast sat beside the highway begging one day as Jesus left Jericho for Jerusalem. Though beggars were common outside the wealthy city, only blind Bartimaeus recognized the passing of Jesus and addressed Him as Messiah ("Son of David"). Though some of Jesus' followers rebuked him, Bartimaeus shouted all the more for mercy. Suddenly, Jesus stopped, told Bartimaeus to come to Him, and asked what he wanted. The blind beggar didn't waste time asking for money. He wanted to see and he said so! Jesus replied, "Your faith [which was the means, not the cause of the miracle] has healed you!" Immediately blind Bartimaeus could see, and he followed Jesus. Many praised God because of this miracle (Luke 18:43).

Helpless outcasts recognized the Messiah more easily than the religious rulers. Perhaps it was because they realized their need and confessed it. Jesus never cast out an outcast (John 6:37), and He'll not cast you out if you'll come to Him by faith.

Consider: *How do you treat people others consider outcasts?*

A Model Sportswriter

Luke   Read Luke 1:1—4

Therefore, since I myself have carefully investigated everything from the beginning, it seemed good also to me to write an orderly account for you, most excellent Theophilus, so that you may know the certainty of the things you have been taught.   Luke 1:3—4

Hundreds of sportswriters from across America crowd the press boxes at major national sporting events such as the Super Bowl and the World Series. Each not only files a game report back to his local paper, but also seeks some new slant on events surrounding the games. Any unique angle makes interesting reading back home.

As a writer who paid meticulous attention to detail, Luke would have been a terrific twentieth-century sportswriter/reporter. A medical doctor who traveled with Paul (2 Tim. 4:11), Luke was the only non-Jewish writer of any part of Scripture. Yet, he contributed more to the New Testament than any other writer. His scientific mind demanded orderliness and accuracy (vv. 3—4). Luke recorded many miracles of healing not found in the other Gospel accounts. Sir William Ramsey, who himself held a critical view of the Scriptures, spent thirty-four years researching Asia Minor and found Luke's writing to be incredibly accurate in detail after detail. Names, places, and events are so precise in Luke's writing that he is acknowledged as a scientifically-trained historian of the early church.

Luke wrote with a purpose: "that you may know with certainty the things you have been taught" (v. 4). His detailed accuracy further confirmed the truth that "all Scripture is God-breathed and is useful for teaching, rebuking, correcting, and training in righteousness, so that the man of God may be thoroughly equipped for every good work" (2 Tim. 3:16—17).

Consider: *Who inspired Luke to write?*

Too Good to Be True

Zechariah   Read Luke 1:5–25

"And now you will be silent and not able to speak until the day this happens, because you did not believe my words, which will come true at their proper time."   Luke 1:20

American sports history is dotted with hard-to-believe events: the 60-foot shot by Jerry West that swished through the net and sent the 1970 NBA championship between the Lakers and the Knicks into overtime; or Franco Harris's Immaculate Reception in the 1972 NFL Playoffs that led the Steelers over the Raiders. Perhaps even more unbelievable was a shot by Les Henson of Virginia Tech in a game against Florida State. With two seconds left and the score tied at 77, left-handed Henson grabbed a rebound at the FSU goal, turned, and threw right-handed, an 89-foot shot that swished the net at the other end to win the game.

Around 4 B.C., a Jewish priest named Zechariah ("whom the Lord remembers") received some hard-to-believe news. As Zechariah performed his once-in-a-lifetime function of interceding to God on behalf of the Jewish nation, suddenly the angel Gabriel ("God's hero") appeared to him. Gabriel, who consistently brought good news to Israel, told Zechariah that despite his old age he would father the forerunner of the Messiah. Even though Zechariah had prayed for a son and/or for the Messiah, this answer seemed too good to be true. Because he did not believe God, Zechariah was struck dumb (v. 20). Only when he properly named the boy John (vv. 57–66) was his speech restored.

Whether it's a long shot to win a game, an unlikely catch against the odds, or the miraculous birth of a child, nothing is impossible with our powerful God. The Mighty One pays no attention to the odds. Simple faith is the only way to adequately honor Him.

Consider: *Which of God's promises are most difficult for you to believe?*

Say Yes to Opportunity

Mary   Read Luke 1:26–56

"I am the Lord's servant . . . may it be to me as you have said."   Luke 1:38

Some athletes react negatively when asked to fill a certain role on a team. These are the ones who do not really serve, but who put self before the group. Others respond eagerly when asked to play a role for the good of the team. They may or may not understand the rationale but have the proper servant attitude, which contributes to a winning effort.

Mary was the type who was willing to do whatever God asked whether or not she understood. She believed the angel and accepted his announcement that she was chosen by God to bring the Savior into the world. Though probably only a teenager, she was the most honored among women, a virgin who would bear the Son of God (Isa. 7:14). The Holy Spirit supernaturally made Mary pregnant with God's Son, the Messiah. Led by the same Spirit, Mary praised God with a song filled with Scripture quotes (vv. 46–55). Though highly favored, Mary was not perfect by any means. She once thought Jesus was "beside Himself" and tried to take Him away from a ministry (Mark 3:21). Mary should not be worshiped; she needed salvation just like anyone else. Her Son, our Savior, was perfect because His Father was God, and Adam's sinful nature is passed on to a child through the father. Yet, Mary said, "Yes, Lord," when given a role on God's team.

God has a role for each of us to play on His team. Is your attitude like Mary's? Remember, God doesn't want your ability nearly as much as your availability.

Consider: *How could you make yourself available to God today?*

Looking Straight Ahead

Simeon and Anna   Read Luke 2:21–38

He was waiting for the consolation of Israel, and the Holy Spirit was upon him. . . . She never left the temple but worshiped night and day, fasting and praying.   Luke 2:25–37

Former major-leaguer Satchel Paige once said, "Never look back; something may be gaining on you." That's good advice in the athletic world. Many athletes neglect defense after a missed opportunity to score; others lose momentum offensively because of a quick score by the opponent; still others look back to past wins or losses and lose concentration in the game at hand.

Looking ahead is imperative in the spiritual realm as well. Simeon and Anna were two godly Jews who consistently looked for the promised Messiah. They refused to let religious ritual detract from the reality of a personal experience with God. Both understood the Old Testament prophecies concerning the Savior and eagerly anticipated His coming. When Simeon saw the Christ child he took Him in his arms and praised God, and Anna, an aged widow whose fasting and praying highlighted her faith, thanked God and spoke of Jesus to all who would listen. In light of the religious apostasy around them, Simeon and Anna demonstrated remarkable insight and patience. Their performance pleased God, and He allowed them to see and recognize the Messiah. What a fulfilling sight for two veterans who persisted in their faith!

Have you been keeping your eyes on the promises of God during the religious apostasy of the eighties? Or do you look backward and get discouraged, wondering if God is really faithful? Fix your eyes on Jesus and go on with confidence. He will surely reward and bless you.

Consider: *What is there in your past that you need to forget and leave behind?*

Reconstructing Your Game

When Simon Peter saw this, he fell at Jesus' knees and said "Go away from me, Lord; I am a sinful man!"   Luke 5:8

Tennis players can overestimate their ability by always playing weaker opponents. Though they may build up an impressive record against inferior competition, they will be disappointingly inadequate when playing in tournaments on a higher level. Only during such moments of truth do players see themselves as they really are and realize how much improvement is needed.

Throughout his life Peter developed a brash self-sufficiency. This tough fisherman from Capernaum, a business partner of James and John, was marked as a leader by his candor, courage, and earnestness. One day, after fishing all night and catching nothing, Peter was busy washing his net. Jesus approached him, got into his boat, and asked him to row out a little from shore so He could use the boat for a pulpit to teach a multitude. When finished, the Lord turned to Peter and said, "Pull out into deep water and let down the nets for a catch." Though Peter's experience made him doubt he would catch anything, he obeyed. Miraculously, a large catch of fish filled both boats. Peter saw himself, as he stood next to the Lord Jesus, woefully inadequate and sinful. Realizing he could not measure up to the Lord, he asked Him to leave. But our Lord had plans for Peter. Jesus called all three fishermen to "fish for men" in His kingdom. The three immediately left everything to follow Him.

Our Lord has a way of getting to us. First, He shows us where we are in relationship to Himself. When we realize our total inadequacy, He calls us and then begins to reconstruct us according to His plan. Once He begins a work in a person, He always finishes what He has started (Phil. 1:6). The result is far greater than anything we could do for ourselves.

Consider: *How do you compare to Jesus?*

The Forgotten Winners

Mary and Martha   Read Luke 10:38–42

She had a sister called Mary, who sat at the Lord's feet listening to what he said.   Luke 10:39

Each January, millions of people become engrossed in the hype and staging of the Super Bowl. Tickets to Super Bowl XIX cost sixty dollars each and the game was viewed by one hundred million people in thirty countries. Winning players got thirty-six thousand dollars; losers eighteen thousand dollars. The NFL received about twenty million dollars; local businesses one hundred million dollars; and ABC, who sold commercials for one million dollars per minute, received approximately thirty million dollars. Although the extravaganza dominates the sports world for a two-week period, the winners are soon forgotten. The Super Bowl championship is so temporary that many people cannot recall winners from even ten years ago.

Martha was equally preoccupied with temporary things. Though a kind woman, Martha was distracted with busy preparations for a temporary meal when Jesus came to her house. Her sister Mary, however, simply sat at Jesus' feet and listened to His Word. The Lord was pleased that Mary chose the most important thing and would rather have had Mary's company than her cooking. The Lord loves our company. He chose disciples so that they might be with Him (Mark 3:14). Our worship of Him must take precedence over our service to Him. Worship is the important and lasting preoccupation.

Where is your attention and affection today? Is it on a game, a career, or another person? Are you caught up with success, results, or performance? Christianity is none of these, nor is it a contest to see which Christian can outdo the other. Christianity is an ongoing love affair with Jesus Christ. Is your love at the red-hot stage for Him? If so, you'll be found sitting at His feet and hearing His Word.

Consider: *How much time do you spend alone with Jesus?*

An Attitude of Gratitude

One of them, when he saw that he was healed, came back, praising God in a loud voice. He threw himself at Jesus' feet and thanked him—and he was a Samaritan.   Luke 17:15–16

How easy it is for athletes, both young and old, to take the blessings of success and victory for granted. We put all we have into a contest, and when it is over we are so elated with victory that we forget to express gratitude to those who helped make it possible. Paul Anderson, the gentle giant from Georgia who was once known as the World's Strongest Man, remembered thankfulness as he competed. When Paul was eight years old, one of his friends was stricken with polio. The restricted life of this young man caused Paul to appreciate his health. In *Out To Win,* Paul wrote that Christians could "stay on our knees for hours each day thanking God for His blessings. . . ."

Our Lord Jesus never ran out of healing miracles. One day as He passed near the region of Samaria (most Jews avoided the Samaritans, but Jesus never did) ten lepers shouted to Him for mercy. They remained at a distance because the law required that lepers stay one hundred paces from healthy people. The Lord heard their plea and told them to go show themselves to the priest, as prescribed by Law for those cleansed from the illness, so they might rejoin society. As they obeyed, they were healed. One man, a Samaritan, turned around, fell at Jesus' feet, and praised and thanked the Great Physician who had healed everyone in a word.

Where were the other nine lepers? Maybe they thought that the one who had given them life would demand loyalty, too. Or maybe they were just ungrateful. Like these self-centered lepers, many people pray for miracles; fewer praise the God who gives them. We must always be on guard against ingratitude.

Consider: *What are you taking for granted that you should express gratitude for?*

Determined Half-Pint

Zacchaeus Read Luke 19:1–10

(Zacchaeus) was a chief tax collector and was wealthy. He wanted to see who Jesus was, but being a short man he could not, because of the crowd.
Luke 19:23

Though size contributes to athletic success, many small people have excelled in sports. Freddie Patek, all of five feet, four inches, was an outstanding performer and a crowd pleaser for the Kansas City Royals during his major-league career. Former major-league outfielder Albie Pearson also starred despite being only five feet, five inches and weighing only 141 pounds. Small pitchers like Bobby Schantz (five feet, seven inches, 153 pounds) have enjoyed great success against much bigger hitters in professional baseball. In almost every case, the smaller person had to offset the disadvantage with extra toughness and determination.

Zacchaeus had the same size problem as these major-league stars, so he had to compensate with a little extra desire. This determined half-pint was a chief tax collector in Jericho. Since it was common for Jews who worked for Rome to overcollect from their own countrymen, Zacchaeus more than likely was quite unpopular with the people gathered to see Jesus. Yet Zacchaeus was determined to see Him. Luke 19:6 records that he welcomed Jesus gladly ("with an attitude of joy"). Jesus must have smiled as He passed through Jericho, looked up, and saw Zacchaeus sitting in a sycamore tree so he could see. Jesus called him to come down and went to his house for lunch. There Zacchaeus was born again, and his life took a new direction. When he reappeared to the muttering crowd, he offered restitution for defrauding the people (v. 8).

Evidently Zacchaeus found no lasting satisfaction in financial corruption and materialism; he desired mercy instead, and he didn't let size keep him from the only one who could give it.

Consider: *What keeps you from seeing Jesus?*

Giving Up Greed

A Generous Widow   Read Luke 21:1–4

". . . this poor widow has put in more than all the others."   Luke 21:3

Greed threatens to ruin professional baseball as owners fork out enormous salaries in an attempt to buy a championship. Such investments are not working, however. Teams lost from 80 to 100 million dollars in 1984. Only one World Series Champion is crowned each year, yet players continue to demand more, as union activity, free agency, arbitration, and the threat of strikes have become a way of life. In 1985, despite a five-year, nine-million-dollar contract, one player voted with his teammates to strike.

Although our way is to get all we can, God's principle is for us to give all we can. One day in the temple Jesus watched people make contributions to charity. Some gave large sums, dropping the coins with a loud clang to attract attention (Matt. 6:1–4). But Jesus noticed one poor widow who gave all she had—two small coins worth a fraction of a cent. He called His disciples together and told them that the widow had, as far as God was concerned, given more than all the rest. Her sacrificial attitude contrasted with the greed of others and illustrated the attitude of total self-giving that Jesus wanted all His followers to learn.

How and with what attitude do you give to God? Do you first give *yourself* to God, knowing that He desires you more than He desires your money? (2 Cor. 8:5). Do you give *wisely* through organizations that are faithful to God's Word? Do you give *sacrificially*, trusting God to provide personal needs? Do you give *joyfully*, with no strings attached and with *gratitude* that you can contribute to the advancement of His kingdom? God no longer dictates how much we should give; He leaves that to us (2 Cor. 9:6–10). But He does look at how much we keep for ourselves because it reveals whether we are worshiping God or self.

Consider: *What attitudes does the Lord desire concerning giving and receiving?*

Last-Minute Victory

Dying Thief   Read Luke 23:26–43

Then he said, "Jesus, remember me when you come into your kingdom."
Luke 23:42

The 1984 Boston College-Miami football game appeared to have been decided when the Hurricanes took a 45–41 fourth-quarter lead in Miami's Orange Bowl. Both teams had performed magnificently, Miami led by All-American Bernie Kosar and BC led by Heisman Trophy winner-to-be Doug Flute. With the ball on the Miami forty-eight-yard line, the Eagles lined up for one last try. With only six seconds remaining, nothing short of a miracle could save Boston College. Boston got its miracle when receiver Gerald Phelan outjumped four other players, caught Flute's desperation pass on the four-yard line, and leaned into the end zone for the winning touchdown for Boston.

The game also appeared to be over for a thief hanging on a cross near the cross of Christ in 33 A.D. The man had committed a capital offense punishable by death, and he knew it. At first, he joined the others in taunting Jesus (Matt. 27:44), but as the hours passed he realized Jesus was not dying for His own sins. He understood that Christ was dying for him! Just before his death, the man repented and asked Christ for salvation. Though unfit to live on earth, he went to be with the Lord that day. Christ demanded no ritual, sacrament, nor church membership of this man. He was translated from sinner to saint by a word from the Master, who had power to save even in His weakest moment.

Procrastination is dangerous. It was fatal for the other thief; he evidently died and went to hell. But if you can read these words, it's not too late for you. As Yogi Berra put it, "The game's not over until it's over!" Trust Christ and be included on His team for all eternity.

Consider: *If the game of life were to end for you today, would you be on the winning team?*

The Song of an Unsung Hero

Andrew   Read John 1:35–42

The first thing Andrew did was to find his brother Simon and tell him, "We have found the Messiah."   John 1:41

For every acknowledged hero on the athletic field, there are many silent types doing their parts behind the scenes to make team success possible. Someone dishes out the assists to the big scorer underneath the basket, provides an unseen block for the flashy running back to score a touchdown, or consistently makes the routine play so the star pitcher is a winner. This humble, supporting cast is usually unappreciated by everyone, except those who really know the game.

Such a man was Andrew ("manliness"). This humble fisherman, who was the first to proclaim Jesus as "Messiah," became the first missionary as he brought his brother Simon Peter to Jesus. He didn't immediately travel around the world preaching to vast crowds, but he simply shared Christ one-on-one right where he was with the one closest to him. Though not much is written about Andrew, his lifestyle was one of continually bringing others to Christ. In John 6, he resourcefully brings a boy with a small lunch to the Lord. In John 12, he is helping some Greeks to see Jesus. Willing to place self third behind God and others, Andrew served the Lord silently as his brother Peter became a prominent leader in the early church. Tradition says he was eventually crucified on an X-shaped cross because of his witness for Christ.

Believers owe much to millions of unsung heroes like Andrew, who faithfully share one-on-one with those who need Christ. They may be unhonored and overlooked today, but the Lord, who knows all, will someday richly reward these unsung heroes of faith.

Consider: *Could you be satisfied if you were called on to be an unsung hero?*

Straight as an Arrow

Nathanael   Read John 1:43–51

When Jesus saw Nathanael approaching, he said of him, "Here is a true Israelite, in whom there is nothing false."   John 1:47

College sports recently have been rocked to the foundations with disclosures of cheating by coaches and alumni. The University of New Mexico basketball coaches were dismissed in the early eighties for academic fraud, five Pac-10 schools got probation in football for similar deceit, and the Florida football program was found guilty of a number of NCAA violations. Dishonesty has been discovered all over the country. The future of college sports is in jeopardy and can be saved only by men who are above such deceit.

Nathanael was such a man. Along with his friend Philip, Nathanael probably spent hours studying Scripture for details about the Messiah. Though he eagerly anticipated Israel's king, when Philip told him the Messiah had come from Nazareth, Nathanael was skeptical (v. 46). Nevertheless, the Lord Jesus recognized Nathanael as "guileless" when they met (v. 47). He was no hypocrite who spoke one way and lived another. Notice, Jesus did not say he had no faults (guiltless), but that he had nothing false in him (guileless). Our Lord knew Nathanael had spent time in private prayer (v. 48). Recognizing Christ's omniscience, perceptive Nathanael made a great declaration: "Rabbi, you are the Son of God; you are the King of Israel." Jesus then promised that in the future Nathanael would see even more evidence for his faith.

Our Lord knows the depth of your commitment. Could He call you guileless or say there was no falsity in you as He said of Nathanael? He sees us all in our private places and knows every thought and motive! That is a comforting thought—for those as straight as Nathanael.

Consider: *What areas in your life would you describe as hypocritical?*

A Step at a Time

Now there was a man of the Pharisees named Nicodemus, a member of
the Jewish ruling council. He came to Jesus at night. . . .   John 3:1–2

Watson Spoelstra, sportswriter for the *Detroit News,* had
become very affluent in his career in 1957. He was a good writer,
but a drinking habit had "gotten out of hand." When his daughter
suffered a brain hemorrhage, he took a step toward God. "You do
something about Ann, and I'll let you do something about me," he
prayed. Later he wrote, "That in substance is what I said. But with
that little feeble half-step that I took, He reached out and touched
me, and I knew at that moment that somehow my life was going to
change and be different, and it did." Spoelstra has been uniquely
used to provide Baseball Chapel to professional ballplayers.

Nicodemus was another "up and outer" who became a
disciple of Jesus. He was a member of the Sanhedrin, a council of
seventy outstanding Jews responsible for religious decisions and
(under Rome) the civil rule of Israel. A nationally known teacher and
scholar, Nicodemus secretly approached the Lord one night. Jesus'
radical statements (v. 3) soon made him aware that he was talking
with the Deity, not just another teacher. Nicodemus was "born
again" and his life was changed. He later defended Jesus at a
Jewish meeting (John 7:50–51), and he identified totally with the
Christ when he brought seventy-five pounds of spices and helped
Joseph of Arimathea bury the Lord (John 19:38–39).

Great commitments sometimes rise from small beginnings.
No one becomes a Billy Graham overnight. The path to bold
servanthood is traveled a step at a time. By simply taking the next
step, both Watson Spoelstra and Nicodemus eventually became
"out and out" for Christ in their areas of influence. The same will
happen to you as you trust Christ a step at a time.

Consider: *What is the next step of faith that you should take?*

Taking a Back Seat

John the Baptist   Read John 3:22–36

"He must become greater; I must become less."   John 3:30

Many famous athletes have given up wealth and prestige to serve in a project where they felt God would use them in a greater way. One such well-known competitor was Charles T. Studd, captain of the Cambridge XI cricket team in England a century ago. Studd gave away much wealth and led a group called the Cambridge Seven to China to share Christ. His motto became, "If Jesus Christ be God and died for me, then no sacrifice can be too great for me to make for Him." He was certainly a man who was willing to decrease his personal gain so the cause of Christ might increase.

John the Baptist had the same self-sacrificing attitude about his Lord. A model for any preacher or teacher, John saw Jesus for himself before he began pointing Him out to others. This forerunner of Messiah spoke plainly about Jesus being the "bridegroom" for whom the "bride" (all believers) was waiting. He continually and earnestly claimed to be only a "voice" (John 1:23) to announce Christ's coming. Willing to take a back seat to the Lord, John joyfully watched as his own followers left him to rally around Jesus. What a contrast to the high-pressured salesmanship designed to build a personal following found in many religious organizations today!

What is your attitude toward prestige, power, and wealth? Are you willing to settle for second place in these areas for the sake of the gospel of Christ? How much would you give up to be used by God in a greater way? It was Jim Elliot, a missionary martyred by the Auca Indians of South America, who wrote, "He is no fool who gives what he cannot keep to gain what he cannot lose." Elliot, Studd, and John the Baptist lived that statement and we can, too.

Consider: *What has God asked you to give up to serve Christ?*

When the Thrill of Victory Wears Off

Samaritan Woman   Read John 4:1–42

The woman said to him, "Sir, give me this water so that I won't get thirsty and have to keep coming here to draw water."   John 4:15

All of us try to find fulfillment in life, but we soon discover that the best this life has to offer leaves us empty. Playing professional sports is a dream for many, but discontentment among players reveals that it doesn't provide ultimate satisfaction. Winning a championship is great, but the title is always up for grabs again next year. The prestige that comes with victory is thrilling, but it provides no permanent fulfillment.

A woman from Samaria knew all about unfulfillment. Jesus came near her town on His way to Galilee. This was not a common route, since much animosity existed between Jews and Samaritans. Fatigued from His travels, He stopped at a well for a drink. Most women came in groups to wash clothes, draw water, and talk, but this woman was a social outcast, so she came alone in the heat of the day. Jesus shocked her when He asked her for a drink. The prejudices of the day prohibited public conversation between men and women, Jews and Samaritans, and strangers. Using physical thirst as a topic of conversation, He got her to admit the need in her heart. At first she tried to divert the conversation away from her sin (adultery) to a discussion of where to worship, but Jesus steered it back to Himself, plainly telling her that He was the Christ (v. 26). She listened, believed, and for the first time found satisfaction for her soul. Forgetting her water jar, she rushed home in excitement to tell what Jesus had told her. Many Samaritans believed that day because of one woman's witness.

Have you tasted the living water and had your inner needs satisfied? Money, prestige, and championships are a poor substitute for a relationship with Christ. Only He can quench the thirst of a dry, parched soul.

Consider: *Where are you looking to find satisfaction?*

102

For the Good of the Team

". . . but this happened so that the work of God might be displayed in his life."   John 9:3

Most coaches have a reason for how they do things. In fact, to succeed in coaching, a well-developed plan is essential. In making out a baseball line-up card, the coach must evaluate the strengths and weaknesses of each hitter and place them in the line-up accordingly. Players who happily accept their place in the batting order are a joy to coach. The attitude of "anywhere you want me, coach, I'm just glad to be a part of the team" makes for a successful team.

One day Jesus and the disciples came upon a man born blind. Jewish rabbis believed that an unborn child could sin, so the disciples saw the man as an occasion for a theological discussion as to why he was born blind. Jesus, however, saw the man as someone needing help and assured them that no specific sin was the cause; it happened "so that the Word of God might be displayed in his life" (v. 3). And that is exactly what happened. Jesus made mud out of saliva, put it on his eyes, and told the man to wash in the pool of Siloam. The man did as instructed and was healed. Though the Pharisees tried to explain away the miracle and destroy the man's testimony, he continued to glorify the Lord Jesus by telling what had happened. He joyfully accepted his role on God's team and brought great glory to God.

God has created all of us for His glory. He didn't create us to build ourselves up or to turn our careers into kingdoms of selfishness and pride. If we do not glorify God, we miss the purpose of our creation.

Consider: *Have you accepted your role and thanked God for it?*

Switching Positions

When he had said this, Jesus called in a loud voice, "Lazarus, come out!"
John 11:43

As players come and go and different needs arise, many ballplayers are asked to switch positions for the good of the team. Outstanding stars like Henry Aaron (outfield to first base), Reggie Jackson (outfield to designated hitter), and Pete Rose (who played almost all positions) have been moved to places where their skills could best be used. Athletes like these demonstrate a good team attitude by adjusting to a new assignment.

A very close friend of Jesus was asked twice to switch positions for the good of the team. His name was Lazarus, and he lived about two miles from Jerusalem in a city called Bethany. Lazarus's older sisters, Mary and Martha, also lived in Bethany, and the Bible says that Jesus loved all three (v. 5). Evidently, He had visited them often when in Bethany. One day while Jesus was preaching across the Jordan River (John 10:40), word came that Lazarus was sick. After waiting two more days, Jesus headed back to Bethany. In meeting Jesus, Martha sadly recognized that if Jesus had been there her brother would not have died (v. 21). Deeply moved at human suffering (vv. 33, 35, 38), Jesus proceeded to the tomb. Commanding men to remove the grave stone, He called Lazarus back from death in one dramatic display of deity. Jesus' resurrected friend came out, his grave clothes were removed, and he became a living demonstration of the power of God, causing many Jews to believe in the deity of the Lord Jesus (v. 45).

After changing positions from earth to tomb and back to earth, Lazarus sank into obscurity. He became a hero of faith not because of what he did, but because of what God did in and through him. The relationship between Jesus and the man reflected glory to the Father, without a word from Lazarus.

Consider: *How does your life reflect God's glory?*

Team Loyalty

Mary Magdalene   Read John 20:1–18

They asked her, "Woman, why are you crying?" "They have taken my Lord away," she said, "and I don't know where they have put him."   John 20:13

Veteran Tommy LaSorda is noted for his loyalty to the Los Angeles Dodgers, the only major-league team he has ever managed. No current big-league skipper has such a record of longevity with one club nor such outspoken loyalty, love, and enthusiasm for one organization. He "bleeds Dodger blue," and wouldn't want to be identified with any other team.

Mary Magdalene wasn't noted for her love and devotion to an organization, but she was most loyal to the person of the Lord Jesus Christ. She had good reason for that devotion. Mary lived in Magdala along the Sea of Galilee. When Jesus found her, she had physical, emotional, and moral problems. The Lord cast out seven demons from her (Luke 8:2), and she became clean—a new person in Christ. From then on, Mary was grateful and loyal to the one who had healed her. She had followed Jesus, witnessed the Crucifixion, and now had gone to the tomb to finish anointing the body of her Lord. Though she strongly loved Him, her faith was shaken when she arrived at the tomb and found it empty. Mary wept (v. 13), thinking the Pharisees had stolen the body (interestingly, they accused the disciples of the same thing). Then the Lord Himself appeared and called her by name (v. 16). A loyal but weak Mary Magdalene became the first witness of the Resurrection. She, in turn, became a witness to the disciples of the risen Lord (v. 18).

While Lasorda's loyalty to his team is admirable, Mary's love for her Lord went even deeper. It has been said that those who owe much, love much. Like all believers, she owed Jesus her very life. Yet her appreciation for what Jesus had done was deeper, and her faith was strengthened by Christ's resurrection appearance.

Consider: *How do you show your love and devotion to the Lord?*

Close Encounter

Then Jesus told him, "Because you have seen me, you have believed; blessed are those who have not seen and yet have believed."   John 20:29

Many athletes have such trouble accepting defeat that they go off by themselves to mull it over. They refuse comfort, even from close friends. The desire to excel is healthy and essential to success, but too much lonely reflection can be counterproductive and unhealthy.

Thomas, hurt deeply by Christ's crucifixion, apparently preferred to grieve alone when it was over. Therefore, he missed the physical appearance of the Lord to the disciples, and when they told him of the Resurrection, he refused to believe it. The disciples had been wrong once before about the appearance of the Lord (Matt. 14:25), so Thomas, fearing pious gullibility, demanded physical evidence. He wanted to "see the nail marks in his hands . . . " (20:25). Eight days later, Thomas was present when the Lord appeared again. Using Thomas's very words, Jesus offered Himself for examination. Thomas's response, "My Lord and my God!" is one of the most significant proclamations of the deity of Christ in Scripture, especially since it was uttered by a Jew. Although the Lord didn't chastise Thomas for his doubt, He did pronounce a special blessing on those who believe without having seen—you and me.

If you doubt the evidence for faith in Christ today, your doubt is needless; the tomb is empty. All anyone had to do to destroy Christianity was produce the body of Christ, but He had risen! The changed lives of millions of people also testify to the truth of the gospel. And in spite of intense persecution over hundreds of years, Christianity is still a vital force, confirming its validity. Why not enjoy Him along with other believers, instead of doubting alone.

Consider: *How do you handle defeat and doubt?*

Bold New Beginning

 Read Acts 2:1–41

Peter replied, "Repent and be baptized, every one of you, in the name of Jesus Christ so that your sins may be forgiven. And you will receive the gift of the Holy Spirit." Acts 2:38

Many college-football programs go through cycles of losing, hiring new coaches, and finally becoming a power with which to be reckoned. Such a turnaround occurred at Kentucky under Jerry Claiborne. Hired in 1982, his first team finished 0–10. Claiborne stuck to his strict disciplinary principles, and in the next season his Wildcats improved to 6-5-1. In 1984, the vision and initiative of Claiborne and his staff was rewarded in a 9–3 season that included a Hall of Fame Bowl victory.

Peter experienced a turnaround in his personal life, and as soon as he got the opportunity he began to proclaim the gospel of Christ. The old Peter had been shifting sand, the new Peter was solid rock; the old Peter had fallen asleep in the Garden of Gethsemane, the new Peter was instructing others how to pray that they might be saved; the old Peter ran his mouth when his brain was out of gear, the new Peter was controlled by the Holy Spirit as he boldly addressed the crowd and "opened the door of the kingdom" for the first time (Matt. 16:19).

What a turnaround in Peter and what power in his message. This temperamental fisherman, whom Jesus had once labeled "dull" of understanding (Matt. 15:16), had a bold new beginning. Scholars tell us that both Peter and his wife were later martyred by crucifixion under Roman Emperor Nero because of their testimony for Christ. What made the difference? The coming of the Holy Spirit. Peter had all of God; and God finally had all of Peter. The same Spirit that indwelled Peter indwells believers today.

Consider: *How were you different after accepting Christ?*

107

Ordinary Players

Peter and John   Read Acts 4:1-22

When they saw the courage of Peter and John and realized that they were unschooled, ordinary men, they were astonished and they took note that these men had been with Jesus.   Acts 4:13

Many highly successful coaches and managers in professional sports were ordinary players during their playing careers. In baseball, legendary skipper Walter Alston had one major league at bat; he struck out. His successor with the Los Angeles Dodgers, Tommy LaSorda, had a 0-4 record after three major-league seasons. Former Cubs manager Jim Frey, the 1984 National League Manager of the Year, never played in the major leagues. Ordinary people who commit themselves to learning the game and handling players can excel as managers and coaches.

Peter and John were ordinary men committed to a person— Jesus Christ. As a result, God directed His healing power through them (Acts 3). An uproar followed because of the many new believers, and the pair was called before the highest Jewish court—the Sanhedrin. When interrogated, Peter boldly gave Jesus credit for the healing (Acts 4:10). The courage of these two ordinary, unschooled men rattled the Jewish religious leaders, and their knowledge, gained by spending time with the Lord, astonished them.

Just as the commitment of a mediocre player means success in coaching, an ordinary person's commitment to Jesus means power for living. For Peter, time with Christ gave him power to proclaim the Messiah to those who had killed Him. For ordinary people today, time spent with Jesus means hope for the future, reproof of sin, and counsel and encouragement for those who are confused or depressed.

Consider: *How is God changing your ordinary traits into extraordinary ones?*

Overcoming Adversity

Now Stephen, a man full of God's grace and power, did great wonders and
miraculous signs among the people. Opposition arose, however. . . .

Acts 6:8–9

Born in Clarksville, Tennessee, Wilma Rudolph was one of
nineteen children. Early childhood diseases had left one of her legs
completely useless. Confined to bed or a chair for two years, she
was given weekly heat treatments in Nashville. Family members
massaged her legs at home. At age six, Wilma took her first step.
Sports caught her interest as she gained strength, and she
eventually became an All-State basketball player. At age sixteen,
Wilma made the U.S. Olympic team; four years later in the 1960
Rome Olympics, she became the first American woman athlete to
win three gold medals in track at a single Olympic Games.
Nicknamed The Black Gazelle, Wilma had overcome adversity and
by the grace of God became a champion.

A Greek-speaking Jew named Stephen ("crown") overcame
much adversity to become a champion in the days of the early
church. This godly man was an outstanding leader of special
servants of the Christian movement. Framed because of Jewish
jealousy, he skillfully defended the faith in a long recitation of the
history of Israel (7:1–53). Leaving out no essential fact, Stephen
delivered his final testimony of the Messiah to Israel. Reminded
again of their sin, the Jewish leaders "gnashed their teeth," rushed
at him, dragged him out of Jerusalem, and stoned him to death. On
that day, Stephen became the church's first martyr, and great
persecution began as Christians fled for their lives (Acts 8:1),
spreading the gospel as they went.

The murder of Stephen remarkably resembled that of the Lord
Jesus. Both were falsely accused; both died willingly while praying
for their murderers; both overcame adversity in running the race set
before them; both gained trophies that last forever (1 Cor.
9:24–27).

Consider: *What adversities have you had to overcome?*

On the Road Again

Now an angel of the Lord said to Philip, "Go south to the road—the desert road—that goes down from Jerusalem to Gaza."   Acts 8:26

Professional baseball is a transient business. At any moment, a ballplayer may be swapped to another team and must move his family to a new city. Many good players have been traded frequently. One outfielder was traded so often that he got the nickname Suitcase Harry Simpson. The all-time record for frequency of trades was held by a pitcher named Dick Lillefield, who was traded ten times in a nine-year major-league career.

Philip was asked frequently by God to hit the road with the message of Jesus Christ. He had been driven to Samaria (a non-Jewish area) by the persecution of believers (v. 4). There he shared the gospel with a group of racial and religious outcasts (v. 8). Things were going well when an angel told him to move again, this time toward Egypt, via Gaza. Philip obeyed without knowing exactly where he would be. God's next appointment for him was on the road. An Ethiopian eunuch (a Gentile) was reading the Old Testament from his chariot, but he could not understand Isaiah 53:7—8, which told of the unjust suffering of Jesus Christ. When Philip explained to this high government official (secretary of the treasury) that Christ was the Messiah who died for our sins (v. 35), the eunuch believed and was baptized. The Bible says that the eunuch went happily on his way, and tradition indicates the great Christian movement in North Africa resulted from his conversion.

If God is leading you to move, rejoice in following each of His steps and remember that this world is not our real home. We have here "no continuing city" (Heb. 13:14). Even Jesus had no place to lay His head. When we are sure God is leading, we can expect Him to advance His kingdom through us as we obey.

Consider: *How would you respond if God asked you to uproot your family?*

The Greatest Arrest

Paul   Read Acts 9:1–9

As he neared Damascus on his journey, suddenly a light from heaven flashed around him. He fell to the ground and heard a voice say to him, "Saul, Saul, why do you persecute me?"   Acts 9:3–4

Today's sports pages are blighted with the accounts of the arrests of famous athletes. Their most common crimes seem to be drug and alcohol abuse. Unfortunately, an arrest and fine don't cure the man, and many slip back into chemical dependence.

The Lord Jesus once made a glorious and life-changing arrest of a man destined to become the greatest missionary of the early church. The crimes of the legalistic Saul, a Roman citizen by birth but trained rigidly as a Pharisee under the influential Gamaliel, began with his active participation in the stoning of Stephen. He then began a brutal manhunt to persecute new believers (Acts 8:3). He destroyed Christians, actually believing he was serving God. Around 36 A.D., his relentless pursuit led him to Damascus. Suddenly a flashing light from heaven and the voice of Jesus Christ drove him to his knees. This revelation of God's glory to Saul caused him to repent. Though he was confused by what had happened, he knew he had met the living God and he responded with submission to His will. Renouncing his former ways, he identified publicly with Christ by being baptized (v. 18). From that day, he became a powerful tool in the hand of the Savior. As John Ryland, Sr. said, "When Satan heard of the conversion of Saul, he ordered his angels into deep mourning!"

This rich, highly educated Roman reckoned all things lost for the sake of his personal Savior (Phil. 3:5–10). Because of the glorious arrest planned by God before Saul (renamed Paul) was even born again (Gal. 1:13–16), he was never the same. Nor is anyone ever the same who responds to a revelation of the living God.

Consider: *What is God doing to get your attention?*

Aid to the Enemy

Placing his hands on Saul, he (Ananias) said, "Brother Saul, the Lord—Jesus, who appeared to you on the road as you were coming here—has sent me so that you may see again and be filled with the Holy Spirit."
Acts 9:17

The college-basketball world was rocked in the fifties by gambling-related fixes involving many top players and teams. Players on the 1949–1950 City College of New York team, which won both the NCAA and NIT tournaments, were implicated in aiding the enemy to influence the point spread. Recently, players at Tulane were prosecuted for intentional erratic play to "aid the enemy," for which they were to receive payoffs from gamblers. Such crimes threaten the existence of intercollegiate athletics.

When God told a devout believer named Ananias to aid his enemy, it was for a different reason than to collect a bet. Calling to him in a vision, the Lord asked Ananias to seek out Saul, the man who had come to arrest Christians. Because of Saul's background (vv. 13–14), Ananias was reluctant to obey. But God assured Ananias that Saul was His "chosen instrument" (v. 15), so the devout Ananias obeyed. As he placed his hands upon Saul, Saul regained his sight.

While aid to the enemy is immoral in athletics, it was right for Ananias to help Saul because of God's explicit command. He learned to trust Saul when the new convert realized how much he needed other believers. The career of history's greatest missionary was made possible by the obedience of an obscure believer who obeyed God.

Do you have an enemy God would have you show kindness to? That's one of the most difficult parts of the Christian life. At the very least, God would have us pray for our enemies (Matt. 5:43–48). When we obey Him in this, it becomes hard for us to hate them, and often we turn enemies into good friends.

Consider: *What can you do today to turn an enemy into a friend?*

Dramatic Turnaround

Paul _____ Read Acts 9:19–31

At once he began to preach in the synagogues that Jesus is the Son of God.
Acts 9:20

Georgetown's Fred Brown was the goat in the 1982 NCAA finals versus North Carolina. At a crucial point late in the game, he inadvertently passed the ball to an opposing player. His mistake lost the national championship for his team. Rather than berate him, however, coach John Thompson hugged him in compassion. Two years later Brown helped lead Georgetown to an 84–75 win over Houston for Georgetown's first national title. The compassion of a wise coach helped transform a player into a hero.

The life of Saul, a legalistic Pharisee who hated Christians, took a dramatic turn when he met a compassionate Master Coach on the road to Damascus. On his way to the city to hunt suspected Christians, Saul's life was changed. Even his Jewish name, Saul ("desired"), was changed to Paul ("small one"). After three years in Arabia and Damascus, Paul returned to Jerusalem and preached the gospel he had set out to destroy (1:15–18). His life was filled with adventure, heavy responsibility, and severe suffering. Ancient writings reveal that Paul was less than five feet tall. He was broad-shouldered, had a thick beard, and suffered from premature baldness. His enemies called his bodily presence unimpressive (2 Cor. 10:10). Five times he was whipped brutally and thrice beaten with rods. He was shipwrecked and stoned (2 Cor. 11:24–29). Though he described himself as weak (1 Cor. 2:3), he lived in victory (Rom. 8:28–39).

Have you ever thought it was too late to turn around in life? It wasn't too late for Saul and it's not for you either. No matter how sinful or frustrating the past, a compassionate Savior still extends a gracious offer of forgiveness, restoration, and purpose. Your greatest turnaround can be today!

Consider: *What area of your life needs a turnaround today?*

The Personal Touch

Cornelius   Read Acts 10:1–48

Then Peter began to speak: "I now realize how true it is that God does not show favoritism but accepts men from every nation who fear him and do what is right."   Acts 10:34–35

After the 1983 baseball season, outfielder Darrell Evans became a free agent so he could sign a contract with any of several major-league clubs. Many teams sought his services, but Evans signed with Detroit because Tiger Manager Sparky Anderson gave him personal attention. According to Evans, Anderson was "the only manager interested enough to call me and talk personally."

Cornelius, a tough Roman centurion, became the object of God's personal attention in Caesarea during the days of the early church. He was a devout man who had forsaken pagan deities and now worshiped the true God. One day the Lord sent an angel to him with a message that he was to send for Peter, who was in Joppa, a city about thirty miles away. Then God gave Peter a supernatural vision (vv. 9–16). He was taught that no food was unclean and that salvation was for all men, not Jews only. When Cornelius's messengers arrived at Peter's door, Peter obeyed God and went to Cornelius's house to share the message of salvation. This experience led to the salvation of Cornelius and his house (v. 44) and was one of the most important events in the early church.

God taught several lessons through Cornelius: (1) the gospel is for all people; (2) if we respond to the light God gives, He will send more truth and light to save us; (3) even good people must trust in Christ to find eternal life (Acts 11:14); (4) we do not need to become a Jewish convert to be saved.

God loves us as much as He loved Cornelius. Have you responded to His personal attention and signed with His eternal team?

Consider: *What can you do today to show someone he or she is special to you?*

Support from the Team

So Peter was kept in prison, but the church was earnestly praying to God for him.   Acts 12:5

A pitcher often becomes discouraged if the fielders behind him fail to make key plays in a ball game. He may get a batter to pop the ball into the air or hit a routine ground ball, but if the defense doesn't make the play, the pitcher's expertise has little value. Support from each player on the field is essential.

Peter learned that the support of Christian teammates was important in his life. As he traveled and preached the gospel he was flogged (Acts 5:40) and jailed more than once (Acts 5:18). Acts 15 tells of one of his arrests and the miraculous intervention of the Lord in answer to prayer. Herod, one of the biggest antagonists of Christianity, had found favor with the Jews by arresting and killing men like Peter. So Peter soon found himself behind bars. The night before his trial, while Peter was sleeping peacefully (for God had said he would live to an old age), the believers he had helped so much joined together in prayer on his behalf. Acts 12:5 tells us that the church prayed—not just casually, but earnestly—to God for him. The answer was immediate and dramatic: God sent an angel to rescue His servant. Even the teams of praying converts had trouble believing their eyes when they found Peter outside their door (v. 16). And Herod was so upset that he ordered the execution of the sixteen guards responsible for securing Peter.

How faithful are you in prayer for suffering believers? Do you flippantly promise "I'll pray for you," and then mumble a few pious words or forget altogether? Or do you support your teammates with earnest prayer? Remember, when the outcome is in doubt, the fervent prayer of believers accomplishes great things (James 5:16) for the glory of God.

Consider: *What are you doing to encourage fellow believers?*

Fickle Fans

Paul   Read Acts 14:8–20

Even with these words, they had difficulty keeping the crowd from
sacrificing to them. Then some Jews came from Antioch and Iconium and
won the crowd over. They stoned Paul and dragged him outside the city,
thinking he was dead.   Acts 14:18–19

Fans often give their heroes exaggerated praise for exploits on
the athletic field. The professional athlete becomes the center of
attention and conversation after a successful performance. Unfortunately, the same fan is just as quick to change cheers into boos
when his expectation is not met. As a former pro-football coach,
Dick Vermeil once said, "The only thing I can do is win the Super
Bowl. Anything less, then I'm an idiot."

As Paul traveled from city to city telling people about the Lord
Jesus, God empowered him to perform many miracles to confirm
the power behind his message. At the Roman colony of Lystra,
Paul's healing of a man crippled from birth made the crowds think
Paul and Barnabas were gods. The people even called Barnabas,
Zeus (the chief god of the Greeks), and Paul, Hermes (the herald of
the gods), and were about to offer animal sacrifices to them. To
accept such worship and praise would have been contrary to their
mission to bring glory to God. Yet, when Paul referred the glory to
God, the Jews swayed the crowd against him, and another mob
reaction took over. They stoned Paul, hauled him outside the city,
and left him for dead. Whether or not Paul actually died is the
subject of some debate, but either way, he arose and continued to
glorify God (v. 20). The praise of fans or their scorn could not deter
him from pointing them to God.

Are you the object of men's applause today? Or are you the
goat in the eyes of the world? Either position is a trial; both are
short-lived because of the fickleness of people. Be careful to
maintain God's perspective of success, regardless of the adoration
or disdain of man.

Consider: *How do you react to the praise and scorn of men?*

A New Name for Crazy Horse

Peter   Read Acts 15:1–11

"We believe it is through the grace of our Lord Jesus that we are saved, just as they are."   Acts 15:11

Former Pittsburgh shortstop Tim Foli gained quite a reputation for his hostile behavior on and off the field. He would just as soon pick a fight with a sliding base runner as tag him out. He became known as Crazy Horse for his zany escapades. Then one day, Tim confessed his sin and trusted Christ. By God's grace, Crazy Horse found a new life. He was as good (or better) a ballplayer, but old sinful habits fell by the wayside. Teammates and opponents noticed the change, and he lost the old nickname. The grace ("unmerited favor") of God had totally changed his life.

Simon Peter was also affected by God's grace. He loved to talk about it. He also corrected the teaching of legalism that opposed the Good News of salvation by grace. When some believing Pharisees started teaching that keeping certain Mosaic laws was necessary for salvation, Peter reminded the church that all were saved by grace through faith, totally apart from works (v. 11). As Peter grew in grace, he encouraged others to "grow in the grace and knowledge of our Lord and Savior" (2 Peter 3:18) as well. God's grace turned the impulsive, temperamental fisherman into a firm, courageous leader of God's people. Peter soon realized that if God could save and keep him, He could do the same for anyone, so the brawny fisherman wrote two New Testament letters—the first to encourage and support suffering believers and the second to warn believers about false teachers and their teaching.

Have you, like Peter and Tim Foli, been touched by God's grace? If so, the gospel of grace will keep you from placing many outward restrictions on others, which God Himself does not do. Instead, you will seek to please the Savior in all attitudes and actions.

Consider: *How has God's grace affected you?*

117

A Second Chance

Barnabas   Read Acts 15:36–41

Barnabas took Mark and sailed for Cyprus.   Acts 15:39

Early in the 1984 season, rookie infielder Bobby Meacham of the New York Yankees made a crucial throwing error in the eighth inning to give the Texas Rangers a 7–6 victory. Yankee owner George Steinbrenner immediately ordered him sent to the minor leagues. Meacham, a mature Christian, took the demotion in stride. "I don't play for Mr. Steinbrenner or for the Yankees. I play for the Lord," he said. "Whether I'm here [Nashville] or at Greensboro [Class A], I will play the best that I can. That's all I can do."

The wise and patient Barnabas ("son of encouragement") handled people in a radically different way than Steinbrenner. A prophet-teacher from Cyprus, Barnabas became Paul's first friend after his conversion and helped him gain acceptance by the church (Acts 9:26–30). A good man, full of the Holy Spirit and faith (Acts 11:24), Barnabas once sold his property and gave the money to help fellow Christians (Acts 4:36–37). Always known for his patient forgiveness, Barnabas tried to get Paul to allow John Mark to rejoin the small missionary group in Antioch. Because John Mark had previously deserted him (Acts 13:13), Paul said no. With this sharp disagreement Paul and Barnabas parted ways, and Barnabas and Mark headed to Cyprus to share Christ; Paul and Silas headed for Syria and Cilicia to strengthen churches there.

Though they parted company, Paul and Barnabas didn't split the church. Their friendship continued, and Paul speaks warmly of Barnabas in later letters. Barnabas's encouragement of Mark paid off because his young cousin became a faithful servant of Jesus Christ. Thanks to a second chance, John Mark became a powerful tool in the hands of the Lord. Years later, even Paul wrote how useful Mark was to him (2 Tim. 4:11).

Consider: *When has someone given you a second chance? Do you do the same for others?*

The True Blue Lines

Paul   Read Acts 16:6–10

. . . they tried to enter Bithynia, but the Spirit of Jesus would not allow them to.   Acts 16:7

Every year, hundreds of runners from thousands of miles away are attracted to the Boston Marathon, a twenty-six-mile test of endurance and strength. Blue lines are painted on the pavement throughout the course to show the runners appropriate turns. One year, on the night before the race, a prankster painted some other blue lines, which would have led the runners into a dead end. Fortunately, the deception was discovered just before the race began, and the event was run on schedule.

At one point in their travels, Paul and his companions (Silas and Timothy) were about to follow some false blue lines. Coming from the East (Syria), Paul desired to head south and take the gospel to the well-populated and influential cities of Asia Minor. God's Spirit said No! (v. 6). When he attempted to go north to Bithynia, the Spirit again restrained him (v. 7). Left with only one direction to go, they headed west to Troas (ancient Troy), where Dr. Luke joined the party. Not knowing where to go, Paul waited for God's direction. At just the right time, God revealed through a vision that Paul was to go to Macedonia and share Christ. Because of his obedience to the call, the gospel reached Europe, and the history of the world was changed.

Just as Paul consistently sought God's blue lines, we must do the same when we face crucial decisions. His leading is definite and found through His Word, the inner promptings of the Spirit, the godly counsel of mature believers, the peace within concerning a course of action, and the circumstances in which He has placed us. When the Lord closes one door, He always opens another. Best of all, when we obey and follow His leading, effective service for Christ is always the result.

Consider: *How do you respond when God says No?*

How to Use Influence

Lydia   Read Acts 16:11–15

The Lord opened her heart to respond to Paul's message. She and the members of her household were baptized. . . .   Acts 16:14–15

Coaches in America enjoy much influence over the thoughts and actions of others. The opinions of such men as Joe Paterno, Penn State football coach, carries a great deal of weight in Pennsylvania. At one time, Joe was considered as a candidate for governor! Ex-Ohio State football coach Woody Hayes is still a political force who lectures widely on a variety of topics. The late Bear Bryant was one of the most influential men in the state of Alabama during his tenure as coach of the Crimson Tide.

Paul's first contact after obeying the call to go to Macedonia (Acts 16:9–10) was with a woman named Lydia. Finding a prayer meeting outside the city of Philippi, Paul sat down (the proper posture of a Jewish teacher) and told them of salvation through Jesus Christ. Lydia was a wealthy dealer in purple dye, which was coveted in the ancient world. She was a good person, but she was in need of the Savior. When Paul told of the Lord Jesus and His death on the cross for her, Lydia believed and was baptized. The salvation of her entire household followed. She became Europe's first convert to Christ, and later volunteered her large house as a house church, where Paul and his companions stayed on more than one occasion.

Salvation only occurs when God opens a person's heart to the truth. No amount of cajoling by a well-meaning preacher can convince a person to get saved. The Spirit of God uses the Word of God through the man (or woman) of God to open hearts of both men and women to the Lord Jesus. Because Lydia used her influence for good, neither her household, nor the city of Philippi were ever the same again.

Consider: *How are you using your influence?*

Tough in the Trenches

After they had been severely flogged, they were thrown into prison . . . their feet in the stocks. About midnight Paul and Silas were praying and singing hymns to God, and the other prisoners were listening to them.

Acts 16:23–25

No one thought Arnold Palmer had a chance in the 1960 U.S. Open. He finished hole #54 six shots behind the leader. But just when things looked the worst, Arnie mounted one of his famous charges. Hole #1 at Cherry Hills Country Club (Denver, Colorado) was over three hundred yards long with a water hazard in front of the green. The other pros played it safe with short shots, but Arnie went for the green. He drove over the hazard, sank a birdie putt, and finished with the lowest nine-hole total ever shot in the U.S. Open— a 30. He went on to win the entire tournament!

When things looked the worst for Paul and Silas, they didn't quit either. While they preached in Philippi, a demon-possessed fortune teller told people that they were sharing the way of salvation. She was correct, but God did not need the testimony of Satan, whose only motive was to weaken the apostles' witness. Paul cast the demon out of the fortune teller, making the girl's owners furious. They incited a mob against the apostles, who were then falsely charged, beaten with rods, thrown into a dark prison, and put into stocks. Even though this treatment was illegal (because both men were Roman citizens), Paul and Silas responded by praying and praising the Lord (v. 25). Prisoners listened in amazement to men who could praise God in spite of terrible circumstances.

How do you react when you are six shots behind like Arnold Palmer or confined like Paul and Silas? Anyone can sing when things are going smoothly; a Christian, however, can sing when the trial is going on, knowing that God has a higher purpose in mind (Rom. 8:28).

Consider: *How would you respond if you were put in prison for your faith?*

Caught in a Crisis

Read Acts 16:26—34

The jailer woke up, and when he saw the prison doors open, he drew his sword and was about to kill himself. . . .   Acts 16:27

Throughout an outstanding high-school and college career, All-American quarterback Steve Bartkowski developed great self-confidence. He became a proud, self-sufficient, unbroken man. Then, in his first NFL season with the 1975 Atlanta Falcons, Steve suffered several elbow dislocations that finally required surgery. Subsequent knee surgery, erratic play, and fan abuse in his fourth year helped Steve remember a stranger who had once told him how to become a Christian. He humbly bowed his head and asked Jesus Christ to come into his life. "It was a last resort for me," Steve said. "I did not know what else to do . . . I was scared."

God often uses crisis experiences to bring people to Him. Another man brought to God through a crisis was the warden in charge of Paul and Silas, who were imprisoned in dark, torturous chambers, possibly in a large cavern beneath the warden's house. At midnight, while Paul and Silas joyfully praised God in spite of their imprisonment, God rocked the jailhouse with an earthquake, causing a crisis that brought the jailer to his knees. Knowing he would be executed if the prisoners escaped, the trembling jailer asked the apostles, "What must I do to be saved?" (v. 30). "Believe on the Lord Jesus Christ," they answered (v. 31). Nothing more, nothing less. God made the plan of salvation so simple that anyone who believes may be saved. The jailer and his family said yes to the invitation.

What is your response to the gospel of salvation? Do you scorn God's plan as too simple and try to add good works to merit His favor? Follow the example of both Bartkowski and the jailer. Admit your sin, accept forgiveness, and God will save you.

Consider: *How do you respond to suffering?*

The Price Tag of Protection

> . . . they dragged Jason and some other brothers before the city officials, shouting: "These men who have caused trouble all over the world have now come here, and Jason has welcomed them into his house." Acts 17:6–7

Pro football teams must throw the football to win, so the quarterback is an extremely valuable player. Defensive linemen and linebackers are programed to get the quarterback at all costs. The offensive linemen, to protect their leader, form a pocket of protection around him. They take blow after blow from the defense in its mad attempt to sack the passer. The wise quarterback stays in the pocket while self-sacrificing blockers pay the price for his protection.

Jason was like a lineman who protected his quarterback. Paul and Silas had traveled a hundred miles from Philippi to Thessalonica. Though constantly hounded by Jews who rejected the Messiah, Paul went first to the Jewish community. Some believed (v. 4), but others incited a riot against Paul. They couldn't get to Paul, so they arrested Jason, a Jewish convert and possibly Paul's relative (Rom. 16:21) who hosted him. Jason was accused of advocating loyalty to Jesus rather than the Roman emperor, even though Paul consistently referred to Jesus as "Lord," a title that did not carry the political implications of the word "king" to the Romans. City officials collected bond from Jason, and Paul later wrote that Satan hindered his return (1 Thess. 2:18). Though most converts in Thessalonica had been steeped in idolatry (1 Thess. 1:9), they carried on without Paul, who wrote later that they persisted in spite of severe suffering (1 Thess. 1:6).

Jason and others gladly paid a price to protect the one who brought them the message of salvation and hope. Though mentioned briefly in Scripture, he was an important part of God's team.

Consider: *How have you paid a price to protect a fellow Christian?*

Where's the Glamour?

Paul stayed on in Corinth for some time. Then he left the brothers and sailed for Syria, accompanied by Priscilla and Aquila.   Acts 18:18

The life of a professional athlete is not always as glamorous as it appears. Often it is filled with pressure and uncertainty. Relocating is a frequent necessity. Phil Menzie reports in the "Seventh Inning Stretch" that a twenty-five-year-old baseball player who has been married five years and has two small children, has moved forty-two times since being married. The poor fellow must be afraid to unpack his bags!

When it came to moving to minister to the needs of others, a Jewish Christian named Aquila didn't hesitate. Exiled from Italy by the pagan Emperor Claudius (v. 2), Aquila and Priscilla teamed with Paul in the city of Corinth. For one and a half years, they made tents for a living and encouraged Corinthian believers. As Paul's close friends, they accompanied him to Ephesus, where their house served as a meeting place for Christians. The apostle wrote that they had risked their lives for him (Rom. 16:3) as they started more colonies of new believers. When young Apollos came to town, this mature couple took him under their wing and gave him further insight into the way God was working through the power of the Holy Spirit (v. 26). Later, they moved back to Rome for eight years before returning to Ephesus. In spite of their unsettled lifestyle, Priscilla and Aquila are encouraging God's messengers each time we read of them.

Though frequent moves are not always good, they are sometimes necessary to follow God and meet the needs of others. Helping others is probably the greatest motivation to move one's home and family. The important thing is not where we are in God's service, but what we are in His service.

Consider: *How do you determine whether to move or to stay in one location to serve the Lord Jesus?*

Willing to Be Taught

When Priscilla and Acquila heard him, they invited him to their home and explained to him the way of God more adequately.   Acts 18:26

Al Kaline was so naturally gifted with baseball skills that he went from Southern High School in Baltimore to right field for the Detroit Tigers without playing an inning of minor-league baseball. Before reaching his twenty-first birthday, he won the American League batting championship—the youngest player ever to do so. What most people overlook, however, is that though he was greatly talented, Kaline spent hours studying the game and working on his fielding, hitting, and base running. In twenty-two major-league seasons, he collected over 3000 hits, including 399 home runs.

In the early days of Christianity, a Jew from Alexandria worked very hard to improve his skills, too. Apollos had an intellect superior to most teachers of his day, as well as much enthusiasm for the things of God. Learned in the Old Testament, he was a dynamic speaker, who taught accurately all he had learned. Yet, when Priscilla and Acquila heard him in Ephesus, they realized he had not heard all that God had recently been doing. While preaching of man's need to repent (v. 25), Apollos lacked full knowledge of Jesus' death, resurrection, and the power of the Holy Spirit in new believers. Tactfully taking him aside, the couple explained these things to the receptive young minister. Apollos listened attentively, learning essential truths he would use to become a great help to other believers (v. 27). Paul later wrote how Apollos had "watered" the souls of believers in Corinth (1 Cor. 3:6).

None of us can take others any further in the Christian walk than we have been ourselves. That's why we need the teachable and zealous attitude of an Al Kaline or an Apollos. Even though God may have greatly gifted us, He will use us only to the extent that we continue growing in Christlikeness.

Consider: *How teachable are you?*

Watch Out for Distractions

Seated in a window was a young man named Eutychus, who was sinking into a deep sleep as Paul talked on and on.   Acts 20:9

Lawrence A. Keating documented a humorous example of a coach's preoccupation with football. During the 1946 Oklahoma-Army game, Oklahoma University coach Jim Tatum paced the sidelines frantically as the Cadets took a 21–7 lead over his Sooners. Nearby sat punter Charlie Sarratt, his sprained ankle submerged in a bucket of ice water. As the intensity of the game dried his throat, Tatum reached down, took Sarratt's foot out of the ice water, and took a swig. Then he gently replaced the foot in the pail and resumed pacing, without ever looking away from the field.

The consequences of Tatum's preoccupation weren't as serious as those of a young man named Eutychus in Paul's day. Paul was soon to leave Troas, so he spoke long into the night to encourage the new believers there. The group met in a third story room lighted by many lamps. Eutychus ("fortunate") sat listening in an open window. As time passed, his interest waned and he fell asleep. He also fell three stories to his death. What an abrupt ending to a Bible lesson! But the story doesn't end there. Paul went down and by the power of the Lord Jesus, raised Eutychus from the dead. Then Paul resumed preaching.

In our society, hundreds of distractions scream for attention. What is it that pulls you away from a vital relationship with God? Is it sports that distracts you from taking care of your spiritual needs? Or, like Eutychus, is it sleep that keeps you from feeding your soul on the Bread of Life? Maybe a job, a new car, a television program, or even another person keeps you from focusing on what is eternal. If so, determine to seek and enjoy the peace and contentment that comes only from spending time with God and His Word.

Consider: *What are the consequences of becoming preoccupied with "things?"*

The Youngest Player

The centurion said, "Paul, the prisoner, sent for me and asked me to bring this young man to you because he has something to tell you." Acts 23:18

In the dark days of World War II, many professional athletes were called into military service. As a result, pro teams signed many younger players. Several made it to the big leagues. The youngest player ever to play major-league baseball was Joe Nuxhall of the Reds. When he was called up in June of 1944, Joe was only fifteen years old. Yet, he eventually became a good big-league pitcher. He didn't let youth hinder his performance.

Back in Jerusalem, Paul was in dire circumstances. He had to be imprisoned by the Romans to protect him from Jewish religious zealots. The next night, however, the Lord encouraged Paul by revealing that he would get to Rome to share the gospel (v. 11). His promise gave him renewed confidence, but there was another obstacle. Over forty Jewish hit men ("Sicarii") vowed to kill him or starve to death! These men wanted Paul dead and were willing to lose their own lives to take him from the Roman soldiers. They planned to carry out their murderous plot the following day. In the sovereignty of God, Paul's young nephew heard what was happening. Like Nuxhall, he didn't let youth hinder him from doing what had to be done. Boldly, he came forward and told Paul, then the Roman commander. The commander ordered 470 men to escort Paul to safety in the seacoast town of Caesarea.

Our God is sovereign over the greatest and smallest affairs of men. He will use whoever is available to accomplish His purposes in the lives of believers. Despite his youth, Paul's nephew was bold enough to get involved in the cause of righteousness. In so doing, he saved Paul's life, and the apostle later carried the message of salvation to the heart of the Roman Empire.

Consider: *Think of a time when you were called on to do something you felt was beyond your ability or experience. How did it work out?*

The Worst of Circumstances

Paul   Read 2 Corinthians 11:24–12:10

But he said to me, "My grace is sufficient for you, for my power is made perfect in weakness."   2 Cor. 12:9

The faith of Andre Thornton, designated hitter for the Cleveland Indians, was severely tested in October, 1977, when his wife and daughter were killed in a car accident. Had he not found grace and strength from God, he would never have survived. As Andre said in *Triumph Born of Tragedy,* "I have been through the darkest valley, and I was not forsaken. I was assailed by pounding waves and a violent storm, but my God never left me alone. My message is that God can give strength and peace and mercy through the worst of circumstances."

Paul suffered severely as he served the Lord for over thirty years before being beheaded by Nero in 66 A.D. Though in constant danger (v. 26), Paul considered his task "reasonable service" (Rom. 12:1–2). Five times Jewish authorities scourged him. Three times the Romans beat him. Intellectual Greeks ridiculed him in Athens (Acts 17:32). He fought wild beasts at Ephesus (1 Cor. 15:32). And God allowed Satan to afflict his body with a "thorn." Yet, when Paul came to the end of himself, all he saw was Christ Jesus. His concern was not for himself, but for others. Triumphantly he wrote, "We are more than conquerors through him who loved us" (Romans 8:37).

Are you facing severe trials today? Problems and weaknesses are designed to crowd us to Christ, to link us to His power. Do not despair over a lost position on the team, difficulty in finding a job, a problem marriage, an unwanted divorce, or physical characteristics you cannot alter. Like Paul, you can glory in weakness, knowing that God's grace is sufficient when your weakness is greatest.

Consider: *What trials in your life might God be using to turn your attention toward Him?*

Risking It All

Epaphroditus   Read Philippians 2:25–30

Welcome him in the Lord with great joy, and honor men like him, because he almost died for the work of Christ, risking his life to make up for the help you could not give me.   Phil. 2:29–30

Los Angeles quarterback Vince Ferragamo didn't feel like playing, but he took a chance in a 1983 playoff game against Dallas. Indigestion, a sore throat, the flu, and an injured hand couldn't keep him down, as he threw three touchdown passes in a 24–17 Ram victory. "I was sick all week with the flu and didn't feel all that great but it's playoff time and a lot of money is at stake," Ferragamo said. "My hand felt OK but I was a little weak from the flu." The gamble paid off for both Ferragamo and the Rams!

Epaphroditus was a Christian, living comfortably in Philippi when Paul was imprisoned in Rome. Knowing of Paul's suffering, the Philippian church decided to send a financial gift to him. Epaphroditus took the risk of traveling over hostile terrain to deliver the money to Paul. Upon arriving in Rome, he stayed with Paul and ministered to his needs. He "gambled with his life" in the service of Christ and of Paul. When he became ill and nearly died, Paul sent him back to Philippi with a letter of encouragement to the Philippians. Paul played with words in verse 30 when he said that Epaphroditus had risked his life. His very name was a gambler's word. Aphrodite (Venus) was a Greek goddess of games of chance. The winner in dice games was called Epaphroditus (or Venestus) because he had risked hazard and come out a winner, personally guided by a pagan deity.

There are risks inherent in anything worthwhile. But without accepting the challenges of achievement for the Lord and for His people, no one will be won to Christ or encouraged in the faith. So don't let the odds keep you from a meaningful ministry. The heavenly rewards are worth any risk you may incur!

Consider: *What are you risking to serve the Lord?*

Calling Your Own Pitches

Epaphras   Read Colossians 4:1-14

He is always wrestling in prayer for you, that you may stand firm in all the will of God, mature and fully assured.   Col. 4:12

Baseball developed gradually into the great national pastime it is today. The rules are somewhat different from when it was invented. For example, the first hitters could tell the pitcher exactly where they wanted the pitch thrown, and the pitcher had to oblige. Pitchers today not only hide the ball and move it around, they also make it sink, hop, curve, and change speeds. By yesterday's standards, the battle seems unfair to today's hitters.

We can't call our own pitches in the game of life today, and neither could Epaphras. If he could have, he certainly wouldn't have chosen to go to jail. But when faced with the undesirable, Epaphras let God change his ministry to one of constant prayer for the benefit of others. Epaphras, one of Paul's companions, was a Colossian like Onesimus and Philemon and founder of a church in his hometown. While on a mission of encouragement to Paul in Rome, he was apprehended and jailed with Paul. It must have seemed unfortunate and unfair for Epaphras, who could have become despondent and discouraged. But Paul wrote that his "fellow soldier," one of a close-knit fraternity of Christian workers who aided him, remained concerned for his home church in Colossae. He constantly "wrestled in prayer" for the believers there. Paul writes (v. 12) that Epaphras prayed often for the Colossians. He prayed specifically that they would "stand firm, mature, and fully assured in God's will." Finally, Epaphras prayed earnestly, "wrestling" in prayer. It wasn't just a daily sentence prayer asking God to bless the Colossians. Epaphras claimed the promises of God in Christ for his beloved people.

By this same grace, we can accept similar turning points in our lives and glorify God in adversity.

Consider: *How well do you adapt to the turning points in your life?*

The Proof of Loyalty

Onesiphorus   Read 2 Timothy 1:15−18

May the Lord show mercy to the household of Onesiphorus, because he often refreshed me and was not ashamed of my chains.   2 Tim. 1:16

Most fans are quick to jump on the bandwagon when everything is going well for their team or favorite player. But when the same team or player isn't doing well, many desert. As Walt Huntley writes, "They cheer like mad until you've lost, and then their praise will stop." The real proof of loyalty comes when a fan endures the rough spots with the one for whom he roots.

Onesiphorus was a businessman from Ephesus and probably a leader in the church Paul had started there. Possibly, Paul had even led him to the Lord. When Paul was jailed for the last time in Rome, all the others from Asian churches he had begun (Colossae, Ephesus, Antioch, Lystra, Derbe, and others) deserted him (v. 15). Around 67 A.D. when he wrote to Timothy, he mentioned that Onesiphorus (who probably was dead by then) was the only one who had visited and refreshed him when he was alone in prison. Paul used Onesiphorus as an example of the boldness, courage, self-discipline, and faithfulness that he was recommending to Timothy. As Paul was not ashamed to suffer for Christ (v. 12), neither was Onesiphorus ashamed to identify with his imprisoned friend. Paul's low position in the world didn't affect the esteem and appreciation Onesiphorus had for this servant of the Lord.

Society shuns losers. People shrink from identifying with those in prisons, hospitals, or mental institutions. In school, many students shy away from those who are handicapped, poor, or dressed differently. But God's own Son came to identify with down-and-outers. Rejected by the religious establishment, He unashamedly sought out those who couldn't help themselves—the poor, the blind, and the lame. May we do the same.

Consider: *Why do you think some people flee when those who have helped them suffer?*

No Shortcuts to Maturity

Timothy   Read 2 Timothy 2:1–26

You then, my son, be strong in the grace that is in Christ Jesus. And the things you have heard me say in the presence of many witnesses entrust to reliable men who will also be qualified to teach others.   2 Tim. 2:1–2

Pro-football teams know the importance of a back-up quarterback, usually a rookie who can gain years of valuable learning under the starting signal-caller and the coach. This understudy is often talented, but needs diligent preparation, training, and maturity before assuming control of the team. Though the training process lasts longer for some than for others, there is no shortcut to maturity. Only hours of study and practice will condition the young leader to serve the team in future years.

The same principle is true in the Christian life, and all the leaders on God's team pass through this maturing process. For example, Paul found a willing and loyal understudy in the young man Timothy ("God-honorer"). Probably Paul's favorite companion, Timothy was fifteen years old when Paul was stoned and left for dead in Lystra. A godly Jewish mother had taught Timothy the Scriptures as a child (2 Tim. 1:5), and the timid young man was discipled by the aggressive apostle Paul. What a complement they were to each other. The veteran apostle evidently did a good job of discipling his understudy. The teachable Timothy became noted for looking out for others and keeping the interests of the Lord Jesus (Phil. 2:19–22). He became heir apparent to Paul as the organizer, director, and supervisor of the problem-riddled Ephesian church. His availability and teachability made him a successful minister for the Master Coach.

Do you have a teacher who can lead you into a deeper knowledge of God? What is your attitude toward your teacher and toward others who can lead you spiritually? If you are teachable, you have a bright future as a servant of the Lord.

Consider: *Why is there no shortcut to maturity?*

Quitting a Bad Habit

Mark   Read 2 Timothy 4:9–13

Get Mark and bring him with you, because he is helpful to me in my ministry.   2 Tim. 4:11

One of the first responses of some athletes when things get tough is to quit. Whether in junior high, high school, or college, the temptation is the same: When things don't go just as a player thinks they should, he quits the team. One wise father, counseling his frustrated ninth grader about the rigors of preseason conditioning in junior-high football, advised him to stay with it until "at least after the first game." The boy did and had so much fun in the game itself, he never considered quitting again. A healthy habit of persistence was established, instead of the bad habit of quitting before completing a project.

Mark became an exception to this rule. He had been on a missionary journey with Paul and Barnabas when he quit the team (Acts 15:37–38). We don't know his reasons, but it was so upsetting to Paul that he refused to take Mark on their second trip. Over a period of years, however, Mark matured and Paul forgave him. When Paul wrote 2 Timothy from a Roman prison cell, he even stated (2 Tim. 4:11) how helpful Mark had become. Eventually, from information gathered from Peter through traveling with him, Mark wrote the second Gospel in the Bible. He portrayed Jesus as a servant, emphasizing His actions more than His teachings. The dropout who quit the team had been changed by God's grace into a faithful servant of the Master Coach. We benefit today from that change.

Have you been a quitter? It's not too late to let God change you into a faithful servant of our Lord Jesus Christ. Old sinful habits need not hinder you if you will accept His forgiveness and live in His power.

Consider: *If you are in the habit of quitting something before it is finished, what can you do to break the habit?*

Finish What You Start

The reason I left you in Crete was that you might straighten out what was left unfinished and appoint elders in every town, as I directed you. Titus 1:5

One unpublicized highlight of the 1984 Los Angeles Olympic Games was the persistence of one runner in a preliminary race. Though the next to the last competitor was a full three laps ahead of him, the coliseum crowd rose to its feet with a thundering ovation for the overmatched competitor as he strained to finish.

Evidently, God had used Paul and Titus to found several churches on the island of Crete in 63−64 A.D. Despite the terrible reputation of Cretians, many had repented and received Christ. Shortly thereafter, Titus returned to finish what they had started—to organize and encourage each local assembly. Like the Olympic runner, Titus refused to stop short of the finish line in his desire to establish the people firmly in their faith. Paul later wrote a letter to encourage and guide Titus in organizing local churches. All human tradition was set aside as God's Spirit set the criteria for leadership and conduct within the church. Like Timothy in Ephesus, Titus devoted himself to the people of Crete. Though he is mentioned by Paul in 2 Timothy 4:10 as having later gone to Dalmatia (Yugoslavia), it is commonly believed he returned to Crete where he served the people for the rest of his life.

Do you finish what you start or do you leave behind a trail of half-finished projects? The persistence of the Olympic runner and of Titus is pleasing to God and brings much satisfaction to the servant of the Lord.

Consider: *If a person consistently leaves projects unfinished, what does that tell you about him or her?*

Loyalty to the Boss

I appeal to you for my son Onesimus, who became my son while I was in chains.   Philem. 10

Pro-sports have had their share of management-labor problems in recent years. The greed of both owners and players resulted in a strike-shortened 1981 baseball season. The luster of the entire season was lost for everyone. Pro-football experienced the same thing when its 1982 season was interrupted by a similar strike. Disgruntled fans discovered they could live without both sports, while management and labor lost millions of dollars in revenue.

During the height of the Roman Empire, slavery was common. Sixty million people (from a population of 120 million) were slaves, and many were treated worse than enemies. This maltreatment led to many disputes between slaves and owners. The apostle Paul got involved in one of these disputes when he led to Christ a runaway slave from Colossae (in modern Turkey). Onesimus ("useful") had evidently robbed Philemon, his wealthy master (v. 18), and ran all the way to Rome, where he had hoped to merge into crowded city life. One day he heard Paul preaching the gospel and he believed on the name of the Lord Jesus Christ (John 8:36). Onesimus then wanted to right past wrongs, so Paul wrote a personal letter to Philemon, who was also a believer and a leader in the local church. Paul urged Philemon not to treat Onesimus as a slave, but to greet him as he would greet Paul—warmly as a brother.

Your loyalty to those over you is a direct measurement of your loyalty to Jesus Christ. If you are an employee, your service to the boss is service to the Lord. If you are an employer, your treatment of the workers is to be a reflection of God's treatment of you.

Consider: *What does your service to your employer reveal about your relationship with God?*

Big Shoes to Fill

"I, John, your brother and companion in the suffering and kingdom and patient endurance that are ours in Jesus, was on the island of Patmos because of the word of God and the testimony of Jesus."   Rev. 1:9

When a rookie is called to the big leagues, often he is in awe of the players already in the club. Many new players, who as youngsters collected bubble gum cards of their heroes, find themselves teammates of their favorite players. They receive a fresh vision of the men they idolized.

John ("the apostle Jesus loved") wasn't in the big leagues, but when he was exiled at age ninety he did need a fresh vision of the glory of his hero. The historian Tertullian says John survived being thrown into boiling oil before being exiled to the island of Patmos, where slaves worked in the marble mines. It would have been easy for this grizzled disciple to despair and give up, but he didn't. One day he heard a loud voice behind him and a command to record events that God would reveal. Turning around, the old saint saw the majestic sight of the risen Lord Jesus. His robe (symbolic of His authority) reached to His feet (v. 13). His head and hair (representing His purity) were as white as snow. His eyes (which penetrate to expose all sin) were as blazing fire (v. 14). His feet (which tread out all evil) were like red hot bronze. His voice was like the sound of rushing waters (v. 15). His glorious face, shining like the sun (v. 16), compelled John to fall before his Lord in worship.

Sometimes, we need a fresh reminder of the glory of God. As the pain of suffering, adversity, old age, or missed opportunities advance, we must dwell in God's Word and upon the person of Christ. In the light of His glory and power, we must remember that Jesus, who loves us, is sufficient in all things.

Consider: *Who in your life has been an example of spiritual maturity for you to follow?*